A Yorkshire Miscellany

A YORKSHIRE MISCELLANY

by
Arnold Walker

The King's England Press
2000

ISBN 1 872438 32 6

A Yorkshire Miscellany is typeset by Moose Manuscripts in
Baskerville 12pt and published by
The King's England Press Ltd,
21, Commercial Road, Goldthorpe,
Rotherham, South Yorkshire, S63 9BL

Printed and bound in Great Britain by

Woolnough Bookbinding
Irthlingborough
Northamptonshire

Foreword

My father was born in 1908 and was brought up in and around Whitby and the North Yorkshire Moors. By profession he was an engineer but a writer by inclination. He was educated at Barnard Castle School and Leeds University, where he met my mother. For about thirty years he was Natural History Curator at the Whitby Museum and he is still an honorary member of the Literary and Philosophical Society there.

During Hitler's war he was employed in the tool room at Blackburn Aircraft at Brough in the (then) East Riding. He collected these tales before 1970 when he moved with part of his family to Canada, where he lives today.

Delphine Isaaman

Contents

7

The Translation of Brother Jocundus

In those long-lost, pious days before that avaricious old scoundrel Henry, the king, emptied the monasteries of all their monks and treasure, there arrived at the gate of St. Leonard's Priory in York a fat gentleman who was suffering from a severe hangover. The day before he had spent happily at York Fair and, although the fumes of the good English ale had left his head, he was suffering from a fit of the blue devils and thought to take refuge in the Priory against his great thirst and his drumming head.

It may be that he soon repented his rashness, but by then it was too late. With hardly a thought as to what was happening he found he had taken the formidable vows and been accepted into the Order and re-christened Brother Jocundus when he thought he was only being confessed. He was to find that the going was a little hard after his carefree life in the outside world.

The food was not too plentiful and anything but varied, consisting chiefly of coarse bread and a few vegetables washed down with small beer. Even worse than this, they wouldn't let a man sleep. He was constantly being shaken from dreams of roundabouts and swings, fat ladies and oceans of beer to sing at Matins or to perform various unsavoury tasks, which he considered to be more suited to womenfolk than to a person of his talents.

For a very long year Brother Jocundus endured the monastic life of St. Leonard's and, if it did nothing to uplift his spirits, it did have a noticeable effect on his weight. He felt he was being reduced to a flabby caricature of his former fat and jolly self.

It was on another York Fair day that he decided to break bounds, just for a day, and rediscover the lost pleasures of the outside world. With all the cunning of an ardent toper deprived of his sustenance he plotted his escape.

After their sustaining midday repast of beans, cabbage and small beer, the monks took a little time off to recover their energies for the next bout in chapel. The place became sonorous with the sounds of the exhausted brethren trying to catch up with their lost sleep. It was in this hour that Jocundus made his exit. He stole into the Prior's room and borrowed a crown from the unconscious prelate's money box, lifted the keys from the snoring porter and let himself out into the waiting world.

When St. Leonard's roused itself from its hour long sleep three things were found to be missing and not the least of these was Brother Jocundus. The Prior, in a fury at losing his money, ordered his two most reliable brothers to go out and search for the miscreant.

Meanwhile, Jocundus was having the time of the year. The fair was in full swing and he had visited the side-shows, consumed quantities of gingerbread and ale and, when the two bloodhounds from the Priory caught up with him, was going up and down on a seesaw with a pleasantly plump lady-friend on the other end of the plank. He had a tankard in his hand and was merrily singing,

     "In dulce jubilo-o-o

     Up, up, up we go."

When Jocundus caught sight of two grim and familiar faces coming towards him he, thinking it was time to be moving elsewhere, left the seesaw in such a hurry that he fell flat on his face to the accompaniment of screams from his lady-friend. He now found that the good ale of England had taken all the power from his legs but not, however, from his voice. He continued to sing his catchy, if rather truncated, little ditty as the two shocked brothers hoisted him into a wheelbarrow and trundled him off to the Priory.

The Chapter was already sitting, grimly awaiting his return. On his arrival he was still unable to proceed under his own steam and was brought before the outraged assembly, half-seated, half-reclining in the barrow. He smiled benignly round and treated them to a short burst of his song. If either the Prior or the brethren were amused they succeeded admirably in concealing it. The two brothers gave their account of the state they found the escapee in, and the visibly shaken Prior gave Jocundus leave to speak in his defence before passing sentence for the scandalous crimes of theft, priory-breaking and riotous and drunken behaviour in a public place. The unabashed criminal, after a few gentle hiccups and a loud belch, replied, "In dulce jubilo-o-o."

Although somewhat put out by their inability to get anything but hiccups and snatches of song from their fallen brother, the Chapter decided that there was nothing for it but to pass sentence immediately. Quite unperturbed, Jocundus was given the terrible sentence to death by walling-up. A suitable niche was found in one of the cellars and, to the accompaniment of much hiccuping, singing and laughter Jocundus was pushed into the niche with a loaf of bread and a flagon of water and, with bricks and mortar, firmly walled up.

It must now be explained that the Abbey of St. Mary stood quite close to St. Leonard's Priory, in fact they were almost back-to-back and, although nobody appears to have been aware of this, their respective cellars had only a single wall between them.

After a short nap the entombed monk began to come to his senses and to realise the unfortunate position he had got himself into. He began to struggle, so violently indeed that with a heave of his great shoulders he broke out of the wall behind him and tumbled, amid a heap of rubble, into the cellars of the abbey next door.

He was now much recovered, if a little bruised and, as it was quite dark, did not yet know where he was. When he got himself up the cellar steps he soon realised that he must have tumbled into St. Mary's Abbey. He came across several monks who looked daggers at him when he spoke to them but answered not a word. He remembered that the abbey was Cistercian and that one of their vows was of silence.

Quite content to accept things as they turned out, Jocundus quietly joined the community and nobody seemed to notice. So passed another year.

Jocundus, while admitting to himself that it was better to be alive and to eat little and be dumb than to be dead in a stuffy cavity in a wall, could not escape the fact that life was even duller than it had been at St. Leonard's. Shortly after the year end, however, he was cheered by being appointed to the position of cellarer in the place of an old monk who had gone to seek his reward in a higher sphere.

About this time it began to run in Jocundus's mind that the York Fair must have passed without his presence and, if he was not able to celebrate in the city he might, at least, be able to celebrate where he was with an extra tankard or two and perhaps with a noggin or two of the Abbot's Hollands thrown in.

So, having decided on this, Jocundus one night left his pallet and, accompanied by a tankard and a candle lantern, stole down to the inviting depths of the cellars while all St. Mary's slept.

It was the following day before he was missed, and then because the Abbot and brethren were without their small beer to wash down their dinner. After some commotion and banging of mugs and platters, two monks went down to the cellars to jog the memory of the laggard cellarer. They were soon back signing for the Abbot to follow them. As they descended to the cellars, accompanied by the whole fraternity, a somewhat feeble voice floated up to them singing:

"In dulce jubilo-o-o,

Up, up, up we go."

The scandalised Abbot immediately convened the Chapter to pass sentence on the now recumbent Jocundus. Excommunication was decided on, followed by entombment alive in one of the cellar walls. By this time the unquenchable sinner was beginning to get his voice back and, as they pushed him into a convenient cavity where a heap of rubble had tumbled from the wall and gave him the statutory loaf of bread and pitcher of water, he treated them to a number of renderings of his song. Soon the walling-up was complete and the monks retired, no doubt to discuss in sign language the excitement of the afternoon.

It happened that at the time of the evening meal at St. Leonard's, when the cellarer came down to the cellar to draw the brothers' beer, he was horrified and amazed to hear from inside the walled-up niche, which should have held the desiccated remains of Brother Jocundus, the rather faint sounds of his favourite ditty. Back up the steps shot the frantic cellarer, shouting, "A miracle! A miracle!" at the top of his voice.

The monks were just assembling in the refectory after a morning spent reciting the offices for the dead over the body of their newly-departed Prior when they heard the noise. Down to the cellar they all trooped and listened for a stunned minute to the voice from the grave. Then, somewhat circumspectly, they began to pull down the wall and revealed Jocundus, his bread and water untouched, sitting smiling at them in the cavity.

"A year and a day - it is a miracle indeed !" murmured the monks in astonished whispers as they helped the partially sobered Jocundus to his feet. It was decided that this was a special dispensation from heaven to prove the innocence and worth of Brother Jocundus and he was unanimously elected Prior in succession to the dead prelate whom they had just buried.

N.B. This story has obviously been adapted. The story itself is probably mediaeval in origin and is of the type found in various collections of stories such as the *Decameron*. St. Leonard's was not, of course, a priory but a hospital and I very much doubt whether access to St. Mary's cellars could have been obtained from it without much digging. St. Mary's itself was not Cistercian but Benedictine. However, none of this can spoil a good tale.

Yorkshire Proverbs and Sayings

He nobbut sees an inch afore his nose.

He'll mend when he grows better.

He mun have a long-handled spoon as sups porridge wi't' Deil.

He leuks as if butter wouldn't melt in his mouth.

Ah'm as owd as me tongue and owder than me teeth.

Save thi wind ti cool thi porridge.

Some folks niver get the cradle straws off their breeks.

Some women and bees cannot be turned.

Truth and sweet oil allus come to the top.

When whins are out of bloom kissing's out of fashion.

Spit on a frog's head in March and it'll stop your cough.

March winds and May sun make clothes white and maids dun.

Woe betide him in whose garden the mallow dies.

'Tis well to know the differ twixt a leaf and a stone.

Shake a bridle over a Yorkshireman's grave and he'll
rise and steal a horse.

Over much of a good thing is good for nothing.

Promises like pie crusts are made to be broken.

If tha lakes wi' t'bull tha'll soon feel his horns.

If you don't pay a servant his wages he'll soon pay himself.

Why, you're as thrang as three in a bed.

Yorkshire

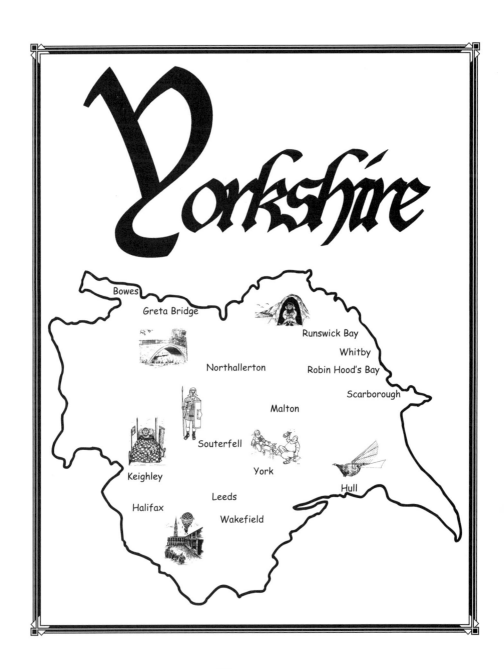

Bowes

Greta Bridge

Runswick Bay

Whitby

Northallerton

Robin Hood's Bay

Scarborough

Malton

Souterfell

York

Keighley

Hull

Leeds

Halifax

Wakefield

Ecclesiastical Arguments:I
The Notable Battle Between the Mayor of Hull and the Archbishop of York

In the days when the Church was still a power in the land, the Archbishops of York, by ancient custom, claimed the right of prisage on every vessel entering the River Hull. This right of prisage really belonged to the Crown and was a levy on every vessel importing twenty or more tuns of wine. The levy was two tuns of wine; one from before and one from behind the mast. It does not now seem at all clear what the mast had to do with it; perhaps the quality of the wine differed.

A charter of Edward I changed this from a prisage to a duty of two shillings a tun on every tun imported by merchant strangers. At any rate this right must have been ceded to the Archbishops of York relating to the River Hull. The Archbishop, at some stage, informed the Hull merchants that they could redeem their casks at twenty shillings apiece. The Hull merchants, being true Yorkshiremen, saw no reason why the Archbishop or anyone else should have any of their wine,

21

money or casks and successfully evaded the problem by unloading their ships out in the Humber into small boats and ferrying the stuff up the river.

This, regarding it as he did as nothing short of skulduggery, made Archbishop Neville hopping mad. For a long time his officers had had the greatest difficulty in collecting anything at all, either in wine or money. The Archbishop made up his mind that unless he took a firm stand to maintain his privileges they would be altogether lost. To make matters worse the Mayor of Hull was, to say the least, uncooperative and obviously had a foot in the other camp. So, in 1373, His Grace decided to go to Hull himself and enforce the restitution of his rights.

The Mayor of Hull at this time was Sir Thomas de Waltham, a knight of quick temper and no respecter of persons, ecclesiastical or otherwise. So the Visitation was made but not quite with the results that the Archbishop, with his train of ten attendants, had anticipated.

The Mayor, accompanied by two bailiffs, John Arnold and Thomas Green, and a large company of local supporters, met His Grace outside the town and an argument soon developed. The Archbishop complained that the Mayor was wanting in respect for him as the representative of Mother Church, and that he was abetting criminals in their evasions of his just dues and talked on and on in top class ecclesiastical language. The Mayor soon warmed up and, growing rapidly red in the face, retorted that he was only doing his duty in maintaining the rights of his fellow citizens. His Grace shouted he'd soon show him as he intended to enforce the just payment of his dues. Then the fun began.

The irascible Mayor noticed one of the Archbishop's retainers grinning at him and giving him a very doubtful digital sign. Without a moment's hesitation the Mayor grabbed the crozier from the Archbishop and struck the man with it, effectively wiping the grin from his face. This was the start of a free fight in which the Prelate and his men suffered a severe defeat. This was not surprising considering the hornet's nest they had walked into, where they were outnumbered by at least ten to one. The church party beat a hasty retreat followed by a jeering mob. The Mayor, it must be recorded, put up a magnificent show, wielding the crozier mightily until it was broken into several pieces.

Of course, such goings on could not possibly be allowed to end there, especially as the Archbishop was reported to have some influence at Court. He took his wrongs and his bruises to the King and the Mayor was summoned to appear before His Majesty at Westminster. He must have pleaded his case very cleverly, or perhaps the King preferred the battling knight to the beaten Archbishop. Judgement was left in abeyance or, in effect, His Grace was non-suited.

After the death of Archbishop Neville it was, for many years, believed that his ghost haunted the place of his discomfiture.

N.B. This is a nice tale but I should say that I can find no definite confirmation of it in the annals of Hull, although there was undoubtedly friction over York's claim to prisage about that time. The claim probably arose from the Archbishop's lordship of Beverley from where the River Hull was navigable.

Yorkshire

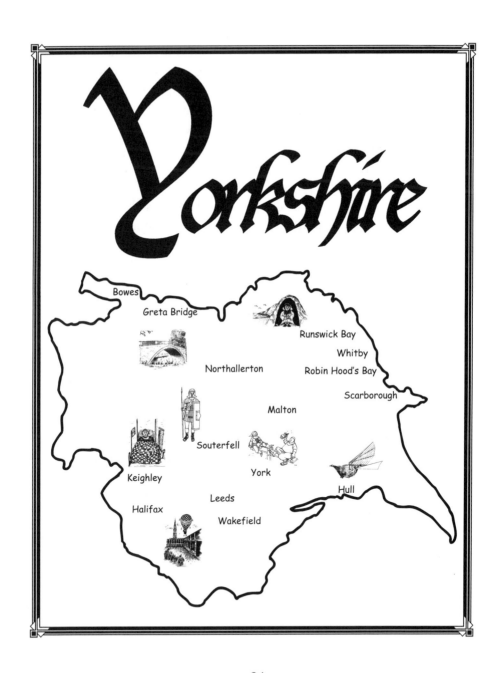

Bowes

Greta Bridge

Runswick Bay

Whitby

Northallerton

Robin Hood's Bay

Scarborough

Malton

Souterfell

Keighley

York

Hull

Leeds

Halifax

Wakefield

A Master of Invective and Abuse

The Old Chapel in Flowergate, Whitby, had been without a minister for some time when, in 1888, the Reverend Francis Haydn Williams arrived to take over the position. The Chapel was of the Unitarian persuasion and had been founded in 1695. A short time before his appointment Reverend Williams had abandoned Congregationalism and taken up the Unitarian ministry. Although later in life he severed his connection with the Unitarian Church, he continued to hold much the same beliefs.

He was a most intelligent, well-read man and a brilliant orator. That he became obsessed later in life and seems to have become a classic example of persecution mania was a tragedy but, until his death in 1910, he certainly enlivened the Whitby district.

Apart from *A Shakespeare Lectionary*, a hymn book and a work called *The Bible for the Practical Man* Haydn Williams was responsible for a vast number of broadsheets and posters, most of them scurrilous and libellous, in which he attacked what he felt to be local wrongs. These effusions include *The Whitby Pedestal*, *The Whitby High Lights*, *The Whipping Post* and *The Whitby Rat Trap*. In all of these, in a quite unrestrained manner, he lambasted all and sundry. As a result he was involved in numerous lawsuits and police court proceedings and, in July 1899, was forced into bankruptcy by the heavy damages awarded against him.

He was greatly interested in what he considered to be the unlawful enclosure of lands and the obstruction of footpaths. With his gang of muscle-men he would, after giving notice of his intentions, stalk up to the Abbey Plain to throw down some of the walls around the Abbey, or go to demolish the railings above the Spa. Due to his frequent brushes with the law he developed an antipathy towards "the Human Blue Devils" as he called the police. Before his expeditions, which sometimes extended out into the country as far as Glaisdale, he would issue one of his notices, such as:

Wanted

Twenty strong men wanted this evening to help me throw down Strickland's stones onto his own land without trespassing. [A collection will be made and divided among them.]

The Strickland referred to was the Lord of the Manor and the stones were those of the walls round the Abbey.

In 1894 Haydn Williams became involved with my grandfather, Henry Walker, over some iron railings he had put up separating the Spa grounds from the roadway above the Spa. Haydn Williams said this was an encroachment on public lands. My grandfather was agent for Sir George Eliot's estate, on which the Spa stood. An account of the confrontation and battle appeared in the *Whitby Times* for July 27th, 1894:

On arrival at the seat of war, Mr. Williams and his supporters commenced operations at the railings opposite the Royal Hotel.

Here Mr. Williams was met by Mr. Henry Walker the manager of the Spa Saloon, and others, who remonstrated with the reverend gentleman and endeavoured to dissuade him from doing any damage or destruction to the property. The appeal was obviously ineffectual as Mr. Williams and his followers proceeded with their attack on the palisading - not, however, without opposition, for a small but resolute body of gentlemen posted themselves in front of the attacking party resisting them, and defending the gates as long as they could. For a short time it was thought that the attack had been repulsed, but the assailants greatly outnumbered the defenders, and the resistance of the later was soon overcome. During the struggle several hard knocks and blows were given on both sides, and some of the combatants are reported to have received various injuries and other marks of warfare.

While the conflict was going on Mr. Williams, the leader of the attacking force, who had previously been using his crowbar against the railings, had that instrument taken from him and this caused some little delay but, nothing daunted, the reverend gentleman immediately rallied his forces and exhorted them to demolish the obnoxious palisading by physical force. They responded with alacrity to this call, and in a comparatively short time the entire length of railing, some 500 yards in extent, was hurled to the ground and smashed up amid loud applause from a portion of the great assemblage, while others gave expression to their disapproval in strong and unmistakable language.

There is no need to go into the rights and wrongs of the dispute here. It is sufficient to say that an injunction was taken out against Haydn Williams and new railings erected.

Williams must have been a considerable headache to the local chief of police, Superintendent Allen. Williams actually summoned him once for an alleged assault on him at one of his meetings. Here, according to the *Northern Echo* of April 29th, 1896, is how that case went:

WHITBY SENSATION
The Rev. Haydn Williams and the police.
Extraordinary scenes in court.

At the North Riding Police Court at Whitby on Tuesday the Reverend Francis Haydn Williams, Unitarian Minister, summoned Supt. Allen for alleged assault while he was holding demonstrations in the Abbey Plain and on the West Cliff, Whitby. Mr. T.P. Hart, solicitor of Scarborough, was for the defence. The court was crowded during the hearing, and the case had a most dramatic and sensational termination. The Chairman having announced that the bench dismissed the summonses with costs as there no evidence whatever to support the charges. Mr. Williams, who was seated at a solicitor's table, jumped up in a most excited manner, and exclaimed, 'Do you think I have told lies here? I will smite him!' Suiting the action to the word, the revd. gentleman then struck Supt. Allen who was seated at the other side of the table, with his umbrella. Mr. Williams was immediately arrested and taken into custody to the cells, amid such a scene of excitement as has never been seen in the Whitby Courts before.

One of his congregation, a Mrs. Tattersfield, was his constant companion and helper in his later years. Together they seem to have become convinced that the police were constantly spying on them in an attempt to be able to accuse them of improper behaviour. As a result of this obsession Williams published, in 1907, a remarkable pamphlet entitled *Pranks and Prowlings by Human Blue Devils*. In it he prints the texts of several letters which he sent to the Commissioner of the London Metropolitan Police Force while on a visit to London with Mrs. Tattersfield. He complained of:

(A) Persistent shadowing everywhere, as recently in Ripon, York and London.

(B) Police detectives engaging a bedroom in close proximity to bedrooms occupied by me and Mrs. Tattersfield, both at _____ hotel and at_____ hotel in the same road. At the former hotel they, last Monday week, June 3rd, to a number of three, occupied the room next to mine disguised as racing men going to the Derby the next day.

Mrs. Tattersfield, being deaf, arranged with the chamber maids that she would unlock her door in the morning about the time when her hot water and cup of tea were due, and on the morning of Derby Day was sitting in bed sipping her tea when one of the detectives, dressed as a horsy man, opened the door and put his head round it, hoping to see me in bed with her. Fortunately she was facing the door or she would never have known of the incident due to her deafness.

There is much more on these lines as the couple moved from hotel to hotel in their attempts to escape police persecution which, according to Williams, went so far as to put some of his things in Mrs. Tattersfield's bedroom. He actually started proceedings at Tower Bridge Magistrates Court which were dismissed. A report of the case appeared in the *Morning Advertiser*, the last sentence of which is worth recording:

"The rev. gentleman then left the court, discussing the matter with the lady through her ear trumpet."

Williams had a rubber stamp made which can be seen on many of his posters. It was about two inches in diameter and was made up of three concentric circles. The outer circle had the words: "Put your trust in God and keep your powder dry." The next: "Oliver Cromwell alias Williams" and the centre held his name: "Francis Haydn Williams".

A footnote from a poster:

> Five shillings reward will be given by me
> for accurate information as to who threw
> PEPPER about when I began to speak at
> last night's meeting.
> F. Haydn Williams.
> 10/1/05.

There are many of Haydn Williams's posters and broadsheets in the splendid library of Whitby Literary and Philosophical Society and, to give a taste of their flavour, I add a few extracts from two *Whitby Gibbets* issued in July 1910. The thinly disguised names can easily be hung on local people of the time.

Bert Badams, a Woslyin GNOME. This little dark beggar was made for mischief by the Power, and a week last Sunday, he had a fine chance of shewing what he could do (or try to do) in that line. The occasion was remarkable enough. On the preceding Sunday I had attended the Parish Church, just before the "first lesson" DENOUNCED CANON _____ as a THIEF and PLUNDERER of WIDOWS and ORPHANS. In the evening I went to the Mission Hall in Church Street where that abominable RASCAL_____ preached his gospel (?) of BAMBOOZLE,_____ took good care not to be there, hence I had no opportunity of denouncing HIM.

A little later in the same *Gibbet* he had a tilt at Wesley:

Jack Wesley's silliness, where women were concerned is seen in the facts (a) that he got into a bad squabble with the Governor of New York because (J.W.) ex-communicated the Governor's wife. When she presented herself at the "Lord's Table" Jack publicly refused her. This led to Jack's sudden return to England. Other stupidities with women may be cited but I will only add (b) his marrying Mrs. Vizzelle, a widow with five children. Poor Jack had to pay heavily for this folly, his wife declared that he had spent HER MONEY with OTHER women, and she sometimes badly mauled the Johnee who founded Methodism.

A few days later another *Gibbet* appeared attacking the local medical officer over the shaking of carpets in the street.

> **Our Medical Officer of Death, Chuffey Chinley, junior**
> This chap is another of the humbugs in office, in our cussed old town. He knows how to TAKE HIS SALARY and to NEGLECT HIS WORK. He was present at the last monthly meeting of the Urban Council, when I complained of the shaking of rugs and carpets in the streets at illegal hours. He heard me tell the Council of my having inhaled the deadly microbe diplococcus, while walking through Cliff Street, where some wretches had beaten carpets and rugs. He heard me relate my narrow escape from death by pneumonia through the skill and energy of Dr. Raw. He heard me cite the law under which the town is laid viz:- All such shaking of rugs and carpets must be done before seven o' clock in the morning.

And so, later that year, mourned by few and to the relief of many, Francis Haydn Williams passed out of the local scene at Whitby. And all those who remembered him have gone too, but the *Gibbets*, the *Whipping Posts* and the *Rat Traps* are there to be read with something like amazement in our less colourful age.

Early Yorkshire Balloonauts

On Saturday September 9th, 1863, a balloon rose into the air from the grounds of Piece Hall, Halifax. It had been named The *Volunteer* and it took four hours to inflate. At six in the evening Mr. Youinge, the owner, climbed into the car and prepared to take off. He was to have taken a woman passenger but, to her disappointment, he decided to go alone. This was just as well, as it turned out.

The balloon was freed and rose gently into the air. The first check came when it was only a few yards from the ground. It had been believed that every precaution had been taken for a clear ascent, avoiding the telegraph wires, the high wall, the chimney of Firth and Son's Mill and the spire of the square chapel south-east of the Hall. It did not avoid the telegraph wires. When it was finally extracted from the wires it rose again, cleared the wall top by the narrowest margin amid gasps from the crowd, and rose into the fresh westerly wind.

There were shouts and shrieks of horror as the swinging car struck the top of Firth's chimney and stuck there, the great envelope heaving backwards and forwards in the wind. Then the strain was too much and the balloon burst and collapsed across the mouth of the chimney. Now the intrepid balloonaut found himself suspended 125 feet in the air with no apparent means of descending. However, Mr. Youinge was made of stern stuff. He took off his topper and waved it cheerfully to the crowd assembled below. An hour later he was still there. Then it was seen that he was paying out a rope and soon he began to descend hand over hand. When he reached the rope's end he was still some twenty feet from the ground and a long ladder had to be found before he could be rescued and carried off to the Talbot to be feted.

On the Sunday a steeplejack named Rawson climbed the rope in an attempt to dislodge the envelope so that the mill fires could be lit for Monday. As he rested near the top the rope, which must have been frayed, broke and he fell to his death.

Another ascent from Crow Wood Park, Sowerby Bridge, in 1906 was more successful. The Prince of Wales was filled with gas from the mains and took off in great style with the owner, Mr. Bramwell, and his assistant Mr. Wood. They are reported to have had a wonderful journey, passing at some thirty miles an hour over Halifax, Brighouse, Bradford, Wakefield and other places. After dark, at a height of some 6,000 feet, they saw the lights of Leeds and the furnaces of Sheffield in the distance. Once they tried to land but had to let out some ballast and reascend as no suitable landing ground could be seen. They finally came to earth near Doncaster, having descended, they said, from 6,000 feet in five minutes.

A curious tongue-in-cheek notice appeared in the *York Gazette* for the 10th of January, 1783:

"Whereas the balloon has been found of such singular advantage in France, in conveying people in an easy and expeditious manner from place to place: this is to give notice that, for the accommodation of the people of the neighbourhood of Whitby, &c, a large balloon is now completed there, with every advantage equal to those in France, which will be found the best and cheapest conveyance from thence to meet the Fly at Northallerton, as the innkeepers have of late been so extravagant in their charges. It will set off every morning at eight o'clock from the Robin Hood in Northallerton, and be at Stokesly about half past eight, at Guisborough about nine, at Whitby to dine and will return to Northallerton the same evening to meet the Fly, Diligence &c., from the north and south the next morning. N.B. It will be very convenient on the Mondays to convey the gentlemen of the law, &c. from Stokesly to Guisborough market and on its return to bring them home again. It will also be very useful for the posts, if they should happen to get drunk or tire their horses, as there will be pockets &c. (and every other convenience) in the balloon carriage for putting in parchments, letters and pocket bottles &c. &c."

The Great Yorkshire Train Robbery

On Friday 11th October ,1867, the seven o'clock train left York for Scarborough and Whitby with the fortnightly pay for the North Eastern Railway officials in the Malton, Scarborough and Whitby area. The money amounted to nearly three hundred pounds; quite a useful sum in those days. It was made up in parcels and given into the care of the guard in his van. It was his job to see that it was distributed at the various stations.

As usual the train stopped at the junction just outside the city and at Haxby. However, on arrival at Strensall it was found that the guard's van was no longer there. Excited discussion followed until the engine driver noticed a light flashing back along the line. He concluded that this must be the guard signalling for assistance.

The train was backed up until the van was reached. Here the guard unfolded a confused tale of woe. He had been robbed and the money was gone - all of it. He did not seem to be at all clear as to who had got it or how the van had become conveniently detached from the train. As the contemporary report says: "Whether the two circumstances have any connection it is difficult to surmise."

The guard's van was rehitched and the train continued on its way without any conclusion being reached as to what had actually happened, but the unfortunate employees had to wait for their pay.

The Tempest Prognosticator

Copy of a letter to the Royal Commissioners of the Great Expedition of all Nations, 1851. Dated Whitby, September 30th, 1850.

My Lords and Gentlemen,

I shall feel much obliged to you if you would provide standing in the building for the Great Exhibition of the next year for a circular pyramidal apparatus of three feet in diameter and three feet six inches in height, composed of French polished mahogany, glass, silver, brass etc., to illustrate my discovery of the means of anticipating storms, to be designated the "Tempest Prognosticator" which I am desirous of promulgating for the first time on that occasion for the benefit of all nations.

As it is my intention to simplify this apparatus as much as possible, to render its operations comprehensible to everyone and manageable by all who take pleasure in meteorological pursuits, I wish to ask the following question: Will the registration of this new and singular discovery protect it from piracy as long as it is in the Great Exhibition?

There will be a pamphlet published at the beginning of the opening of the Great Exhibition, giving the whole history of the discovery, containing

vouchers of its efficacy, and instructions for its management and appliance;
and my belief is, that it will be the perpetual means of saving thousands
of lives, as well as protecting an immense amount of property, I therefore
hope that it will be deemed worthy of a prominent and easily accessible
place in the Great Exhibition.

I have the honour to be, my Lords and Gentlemen,
Your most obedient servant,
(signed) George Merryweather,M.D.

The apparatus was indeed exhibited in the Great
Exhibition, but I have been unable to discover what happened
to it when the Exhibition closed. Unfortunately, Dr.
Merryweather's hopes of a large demand for his invention did
not materialize. However, there is a very fine model of the
Prognosticator in Whitby Museum. This was constructed from
Dr. Merryweather's pamphlet and was shown in the Dome of
Discovery at the Festival of Britain in 1951.

Dr. George Merryweather was a dalesman, born in
Burley-in-Wharfedale in 1793. He took his medical degree in
Edinburgh and practised for many years in Whitby. His curious
and very inventive mind resulted in 1831 in the publication
in the Edinburgh Philosophical Journal of a description of
his Platina Lamp and, later, in the making of the Tempest
Prognosticator. I am not aware that there is any example of
the Platina Lamp still in existence. Dr. Merryweather claimed
that it could be kept burning for two weeks on a mixture of
pure alcohol and whisky. The running cost in 1831 was said
to be one penny for eight hours. With the present cost of its
fuel one would imagine that it would cost a good deal more to
run today.

For use in his practice he, like other doctors of his time,
kept a stock of medicinal leeches for drawing blood from his
patients and he noticed that his leeches seemed to be very

sensitive to the atmospheric conditions before storms. As a result of this observation his inventive mind got to work and the result was a truly fantastic apparatus which he later called The Tempest Prognosticator. It was completed in 1850, the year before the Great Exhibition. He described it as "an Atmospheric Electromagnetic Telegraph conducted by animal instinct".

The apparatus which he built and which was actually exhibited at the Great Exhibition was a magnificent piece of Victorian Gimcrackery - it was also extremely elegant. Unfortunately, over the years the original has disappeared.

The Prognosticator was built by arranging twelve glass pint bottles around a circular base. Each bottle was about three inches in diameter and seven high. At the top they were each connected by a gilt chain to a series of hammers arranged round a bell at the top of the stand. In a metal tube at the top of each bottle was a whalebone trip device which was sprung when a leech entered the tube, so ringing the bell and leaving a visible sign in the tripped whalebone spring. There was about one and a half inches of distilled water in the bottles for the leeches and the only air came from some small holes at the top of the tubes. Each bottle held a single leech.

The reason for the circular arrangement seems to have been for the convenience of the leeches. Dr. Merryweather remarks: "I placed the bottles in a circle in order that the leeches might see each other, and not endure the affliction of solitary confinement." Apart from the indications which the leeches would give to the experienced eye, they did sometimes climb into the tubes and ring the bell. Then Dr. Merryweather would be able to predict a storm. He claimed that the different leeches had different individualities and varied in their responses and that was why he had so many. He also claimed that his leeches came to know him and would never bite him. A noticeable

41

omission from the instructions for running the apparatus is that there are no instructions for feeding his little pets.

The extraordinary thing is that the thing actually seems to have worked. The basis of the idea is that leeches are sensitive to changes in the atmosphere. Dr. Merryweather did not himself discover this curious fact as it was already known. The poet Cowper mentions in a letter to Lady Hesketh that he had a leech in a bottle which was worth "all the barometers in the world". Dr. Merryweather had the distinction of devising an apparatus by which the leeches could signal the approach of a storm by ringing a bell.

During the year before the Great Exhibition Dr. Merryweather ran a whole series of tests and authenticated them in vouchers which he sent to the President of the Whitby Literary and Philosophical Society, Henry Belcher. Merryweather was at that time Curator of the society's museum. These notices begin on January 9th 1850 and end with number thirty two on December 23rd. Two of these vouchers will provide a fair sample.

No.26. Whitby, November 18th 1850. Monday, 4pm.

My last meteorological letter to you was dated on Sunday, 1pm, the 10th instant, advertising you of an approaching storm which commenced at 3 o'clock on the Wednesday following and continued until the next day. It is now my duty to prepare you for another storm. Although it is comparatively mild today I should not wonder to see snow or hail accompanying it.

(signed) George Merryweather M.D.

No. 28. Whitby, November 28th 1850. Thursday, 7pm.

I addressed you last Saturday night, the 23rd instant apprising you of an approaching storm, which commenced on Sunday morning and continued more or less until Tuesday, wrecking a ship off the East Cliff, and causing great disasters at sea, for an account of which I beg to refer you to the daily papers. The storm I advised you of on the 16th instant has been attended with the most disastrous and dreadful consequences on the Western coasts. Although this is a fine starlight night, and the barometer is high and still rising, yet the Tempest Prognosticator is giving signals for another storm which is going to take place here or in other parts.

(signed) George Merryweather M.D.

Dr. Merryweather concludes his description of the Prognosticator by boasting that he could "cause a little leech governed by its own instinct to ring St. Paul's great bell in London as a signal for an approaching storm." No doubt he would have loved to have had the chance to develop his apparatus to do just that.

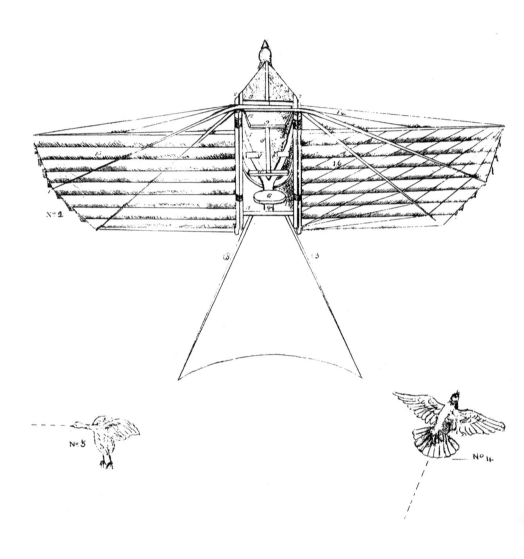

N° 1

N° 5

N° 1

44

Thomas Walker's Flying Machine

Early in the nineteenth century Thomas Walker, a Hull portrait painter, had long been scheming and dreaming of being able to fly like a bird in a mechanically operated machine. By 1810 he had the whole thing worked out and published a book which he called *A treatise upon the Art of Flying by Mechanical Means*, sub-titled *With a full explanation of the natural principles by which birds are enabled to fly; likewise Instructions and Plans for making a flying car with wings in which a man may sit & by working a simple lever, cause himself to ascend & soar through the air with the facility of a bird.*

A large part of the book is taken up with the author's quite acute analysis of bird flight, upon which he bases the principle of his machine. He concludes that the rear ends of a bird's flight feathers turn upwards on the down stroke of the wing, so giving the bird forward propulsion. If this is not what has since been revealed by high speed photography, it is near enough to have given him something solid on which to base his design.

He had no great opinion of his predecessors in this field in which, one must hope, he was not including da Vinci. He says:

"We learn from several authors, in different ages of the world, that the art of flying has been attempted by various means, all of which have hitherto failed of success. When we take into consideration the different methods which have been recorded, we cannot be surprised that they have all failed and they will obviously appear to be nothing more than mere whims and contrivances, all utterly destitute of the true nature and science of flying."

He gives quite detailed instructions for the machine's construction: the car must be made of as light materials as possible and covered with silk over cord supports. The wings are each eight feet long, hinged to each side of the top bar of the car and are worked by an upright lever fixed to a crank. The tail is seven or eight feet long and the same width at the tip. He recommends very closely woven silk for the wings and tail. The silk for the wings must be carefully laid on in separate strips which open as the wings move up so as to let the air through, and close on the downstroke.

In a footnote he suggests: "The tail feathers of turkeys laid close and parallel to each other, and fast sewed upon eight pieces of riband, then extended in the wing, well braced, would perhaps answer the purpose better."

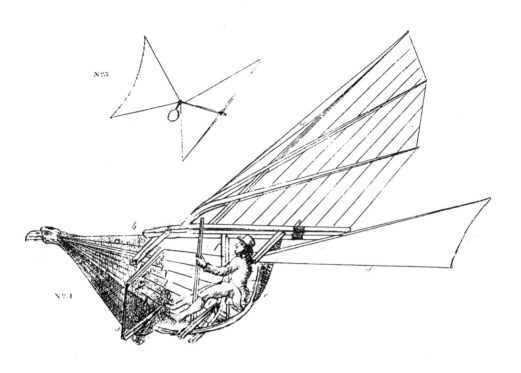

The flying instructions are also quite detailed. The machine is to be lifted onto planks laid across two trestles twelve feet apart, the front trestle eighteen inches higher than the other. The intrepid pilot then climbs in and sits a little behind the centre of gravity. He pushes the lever forward about eighteen inches and the tips of the wings will rise three and a half feet above the centre. He must then, "with brisk exertion", pull the lever back eighteen inches past centre and the wings will "strike" downwards through an arc of seven feet. Air compressed under them will escape backwards and downwards causing the machine to "make an oblique ascent".

Now we are (hopefully) in the air and clear of the tops of trees, buildings, hills etc, and the pilot moves a little forward to level the craft off. "I believe," he writes, "that pigeons can ascend in very near a perpendicular line, but such an ascent would be too incommodious for artificial flight." So he continues working the lever in level flight. To come back to earth the wings are held midway and he glides down until some five or six feet from the ground, when he strikes suddenly downward and sits back as far as he can. He will thus cause the car to alight very gently with a retrograde motion.

"I hope that flying will be of great use, if by such means we can have our letters, newspapers etc. conveyed to any part of the kingdom at the rate of forty or fifty miles and hour, or if a man, by such means, can take a rope to sailors in distress along the sea coast and thereby become the happy instrument of saving their lives etc. It may tend very greatly to reduce the number of horses kept in this kingdom, and by that means a very great quantity of land, which is at present taken up with growing hay, oats and beans for these quadrupeds, might then be cultivated for the increase of our natural stock of subsistence for the population."

Prophetic words indeed, if not for his own invention.

Dickens and Do-the-Boys Hall

When Charles Dickens was researching *Nicholas Nickleby* he visited Barnard Castle, around which several of the notorious "Yorkshire Schools" were based. He got his information for the novel at first, or at least, second hand. There can be little doubt that William Shaw's Academy at Bowes was the basis of Squeers's Academy in the novel, although Dickens denied that Squeers was directly based upon Shaw.

In the original preface to the first edition of *Nicholas Nickleby*, published in 1839, he says:

"Mr. Squeers is the representative of a class not of an individual. Where imposture, ignorance and brutal cupidity are the stock in trade of a small body of men, and one is described by these characteristics, all his fellows will recognise something belonging to themselves, and each will have a misgiving that the portrait is his own. Mr. Squeers and his school are faint and feeble pictures of an existing reality, purposely subdued and kept down lest they should be deemed impossible...

There are upon record trials at law in which damages have been sought as a poor recompense for lasting agonies and disfigurements inflicted upon children by the masters of these places, involving such offensive and foul details of neglect, cruelty and disease, as no writer of fiction would have the boldness to imagine."

Ten years later Dickens wrote in a preface to the first cheap edition of *Nickleby*:

"This story was begun within a few months of the publication of *Pickwick Papers* (1836). There were then a good many cheap Yorkshire schools in existence. There are very few now." *Nicholas Nickleby* had put them out of business.

That there is a strong link between William Shaw and Squeers is borne out by Shaw's business card which agrees almost word for word with Squeers's advertisement.

EDUCATION

By Mr. Shaw and able assistants, at Bowes Academy, near Greta Bridge, Yorkshire. Youths are carefully instructed in the English, Latin and Greek languages; writing, Common and Decimal arithmetic, Book keeping, Surveying, Geography, Navigation, and are provided with clothes and every necessary at twenty pounds per annum each. No extra charges whatever, Doctor's bills excepted. No vacations except by parents desire. N.B. The French language - two guineas per annum extra.

There was an action brought against Shaw in the Court of Common Pleas on the 30th of October 1823 and tried before Judge Park. Mr. Sergeant Vaughan appeared for the father of two boys, Richard and William Jones. William Jones gave the following evidence:

"Witness will be twelve years old in January. He could see as well as any person when he went to Mr. Shaw's school. He had smallpox a year before, but it did not affect his eyes.

The first week he was treated very well. He got toast and tea for breakfast, but then they turned him in among the other boys and gave him hasty pudding for breakfast. For dinner the boys had meat and potatoes on Sunday, and on other days bread and cheese.

When any gentleman came to see their children, Mr. Shaw used to come down and tell the boys who had not got their jackets and trousers on to get under the table and hide themselves; the boys were frequently without jackets and trousers.

They washed in a large trough, there were only two towels for all the boys which the bigger boys used first. Their supper consisted of warm milk and water and bread. Five boys generally slept in a bed, his brother and three other boys slept with him; there were thirty beds in the room. Every morning the boys used to flea the beds, for which purpose they were provided with quills by the ushers, and if they did not catch all the fleas they were beaten.

About nine months after he had been at school, his sight was affected, and he could not see to write his copy, and Mr. Shaw threatened to beat him. The next day he could not see at all and Mr. Shaw sent him to the wash-house as he had no doctor and Mr. Shaw would not have him in his room. There were eighteen boys there besides himself, of whom two were totally blind. In November he was quite blind. Dr. Bennings used to come to the school when the boys had nearly lost their sight. He merely looked at their eyes and then turned them off."

Richard Jones corroborated the statement of his brother, adding that he had the itch all the time he was there.

Twenty other boys had the same disorder. Benjamin Clatton described the mode of flea hunting. There was a quill to each bed which the four or five bedfellows filled and emptied in the fire.

Two medical gentlemen deposed that the cause of the boy's blindness was gross neglect. The verdict was for the plaintiff with damages of 300 pounds.

Dickens says in a letter to Mrs. Hall, the Irish novelist:

"If I am not mistaken, another action was brought against him (Shaw) by the parents of a miserable child, a cancer of whose head he opened with an inky penknife, and so caused his death."

The character Smike in *Nicholas Nickleby* was probably based on an unfortunate boy called Edward Smith, although it is unlikely that it was his real name. According to a letter from Edward Hardy of Woodlands to a friend, Edward Smith undoubtedly came of good parents. He had faint recollections of being taken from home at about five years old and brought to Bowes by Mr. Shaw. The school, which went under the appropriate name of DotheBoys Hall, had a great deal of mystery and secrecy attached to it, and was for the sole purpose of rearing boys and girls in total ignorance of who their parents were.

When they were old enough to work, they were sent to various employments. Shaw kept a farm and when Neddy was old enough he worked there as a farm servant until he was 21 years old. Then he came to Woodlands and remained in the neighbourhood until he died about 1885.

The next time you pass through Bowes and see the sign for Dotheboys Hall, think of Neddy Smith and Richard and William Jones and Benjamin Clatton and the hundreds of other children who lived a lost and abominably miserable life there, with no hope of escape.

More Yorkshire Proverbs and Sayings

A given bite is soon put out of sight.

As queer as Dick's hatband 'at went nine times roond and wouldna tee.

As deead as a doar nail.

A geen horse suddn't be leuked in t'mouth.

An ill servant will niver mak a good maister.

As nimble as a cow in a cage.

As threng as Thrap's wife when she henged hersel' in her garters.

Attorney's houses are built on t'heeads o' fools.

As nimble as a cat on a hot backstone.

After wait comes ower late.

As angry as if he'd sat bare backside on a nettle.

Better rue sell as rue keep.

Every bird mun hetch her ain eggs.

Fouls words breeak ni bones.

Give a Yorkshireman a bridle and he'll steal a horse.

From Hull, Hell and Halifax good Lord deliver us.
(Said to refer to the Halifax gibbet.)

He leuks as grue as thunder.

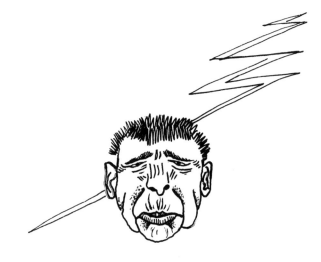

54

The Yorkshire Odysseus

History does not tell us how or why Sir William Wentworth Blackett became obsessed with the idea that the world was flat, and that somewhere there was a World's End which he had to find.

Sir William was Squire of Bretton Hall near Wakefield and, despite the arguments and tears of his loving wife, decided he must go on a quest across the flat world and find out where it ended.

By sea and land he travelled, facing hardship and danger with the dedication of a fanatic until, after over twenty years, he had neither fallen off the world nor been able to discover any confirmation of his beliefs.

Finally, an old shipmaster in a foreign port convinced him that he had been on a fool's errand and that the world wasn't really flat after all. He began to think of his wife and set off for England.

At Bretton Hall, while her husband had been roaming the world for all this time, his poor deserted wife had had no news of him. Finally she became convinced that he must be dead and she agreed to marry a local gentleman who had been wooing her for some years.

As the homebound traveller came to Wakefield he heard of the impending marriage and determined to put a spoke in the wheel of the man who was trying to steal his wife. His travels had left him tanned and weather-beaten and he dressed himself as a beggar and arrived at Bretton Hall on the very day of the wedding.

He knocked on the door and asked for charity but the servants gave him nothing but a crust of bread. He asked for beer and the servants called him saucy, drunken vagabond and told him to take himself off. He persisted, and after much argument did get a pot of beer. He quaffed it off, gave back the pot and strode into the Hall, saying he wished to speak to her ladyship. The servants told him that she was newly married and attempted to evict him but he forced his way into the banqueting hall with the clamorous servants all around him making such a commotion that her ladyship came to see what was the matter.

When Sir William saw his wife he asked for a glass of wine to drink her health, but she refused as she did not recognise him.

However, her husband was not to be denied. He pushed past her and, seating himself among the guests, proceeded to pour himself glass after glass of wine and then made a great commotion by going to his wife, throwing his arms round her neck and kissing her. When she threatened to have him forcibly removed he laughed and said, "Madam, it is your new bridegroom who will be thrown out tonight for I intend to take his place."

At this the bridegroom and the guests arose as one man with the intention of ridding themselves of this unwelcome intruder. So there was nothing for it but that Sir William should make himself known - to the amazement of all and the chagrin of the ousted bridegroom.

When the lady realised that this was indeed her long-lost husband, she flew into his arms and begged his forgiveness. He freely forgave her and they lived happily ever after.

It is said that the boots and old hat in which Sir William returned from his voyaging were kept as a memento at Bretton Hall.

From an old Broadsheet

The Hand of Glory

The Spital Inn on Stainmoor was mentioned in connection with the Siege of Forcegarth. The Inn itself is one of the places where an attack by robbers using the Hand of Glory is reported. The belief of criminals, that the Hand of Glory would make their job easier by magically putting the occupants of a house into some kind of deep sleep or trance from which they could not be wakened until the robbery was over, may well have been believed in the 1790s when the attack on the Spital Inn is said to have taken place.

The Hand was to be taken at the wrist from an executed criminal on a gibbet and carefully dried and mummified with the fingers and thumb curled round in such a way as to make a candlestick. There is a second type recorded where the fingers and thumb were soaked in wax so that they could be lighted. In the no doubt embroidered tale of the attack on the Spital Inn a candle was used in the hand.

Late one evening when the landlord, George Alderson, and his family were sitting round the fire there was a loud knocking at the door and he sent the servant girl to see who it was. She unbarred and unlocked the door, leaving it on the chain until she could see who was there. What she saw was an old, bent woman in a long skirt, who begged to be allowed in as the night was turning stormy. The landlord agreed to this and she came in and was given a seat by the fire.

The landlord and his family went upstairs to bed and the servant girl prepared to sleep as usual on a long settle while the 'old woman' remained seated by the fire. The girl settled down but, before she dozed off, had another look at the 'old woman' and was alarmed to see the legs of a man's trousers and the toes of riding boots below the person's skirts.

The girl decided that she would pretend to be asleep and see what the strange visitor would do. After a little while he got up and came over and looked at the girl, listening to her breathing. While she was now too frightened to move she continued to breathe deeply as if asleep. Satisfied, he moved away and took out of his cloak what she could see was a withered human hand. He propped up a candle in it which he lit from the fire, muttering in a low voice:
"Let those who are asleep
Be asleep,
Let those who wake
Be awake."
Then he went to the window, drew back the curtains and passed the lighted Hand across the window as a signal to those outside and, putting the Hand down on the table, went to unfasten the door. He unlocked and unbarred it and loosed the chain. When he had opened the door and was about to step outside the servant girl, with great courage, pushed him violently in the back so that he fell down the steps. She then slammed the door and locked and barred it again. There was a great deal of shouting and cursing from outside as the girl

60

ran upstairs and tried to wake the family, but shake and call them as she would, none would wake up. Realizing that something she had once heard about the Hand of Glory might be the cause, she ran down again and tried to blow it out. But blowing and pouring water on it did not quench it so she tipped a bowl of milk from the table onto it and that doused it. Now when she called up the stairs the landlord replied and came down. When he heard the yelling and cursing from outside and heard what happened inside he called his son down and they took up their blunderbusses. The landlord opened one of the upper windows and told the gang to be off. One of them replied, "Give us the Hand and we'll harm nobody." In reply the landlord's son fired from the window and they heard groans and curses and then all went quiet. The following morning they found blood on the roadway but no sign of the robbers.

S. Baring Gould tells of an example from Northumberland where two "magicians" were foiled when they tried to use the Hand of Glory. The cook, who had been watching them through a glass window in the kitchen door, threw milk over the candle extinguishing it, and the household, which had apparently been fast asleep, awoke and came down and secured the two men. Sir James Frazer in the *Golden Bough* cites European use of candles made from the fat of malefactors put into the Hand; also of the use being made of the fingers of new-born or still-born children.

It is not too difficult to see how this curious practice, obviously unbelievable today, could have been thought to be effective. If the people of a house did not awake for natural reasons, such as heavy sleep, while a robbery was in progress in which a Hand of Glory was being used, the belief would flourish. The Spital Inn and similar examples could well have been embellished with a quick and successful response by one or more people of the house.

Yorkshire

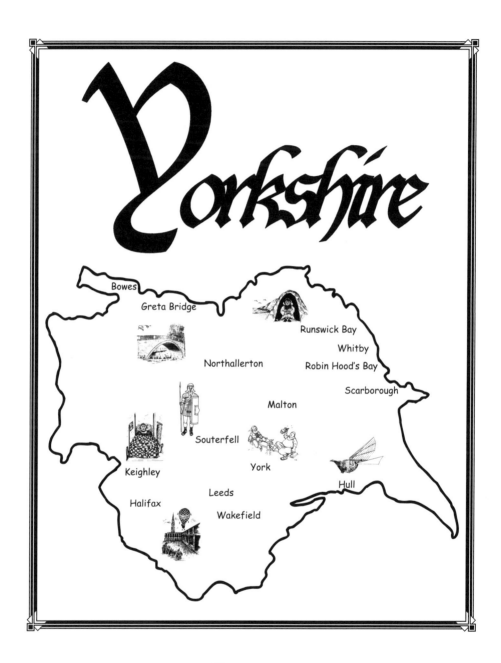

Bowes

Greta Bridge

Runswick Bay

Whitby

Northallerton

Robin Hood's Bay

Scarborough

Malton

Souterfell

Keighley

York

Hull

Leeds

Halifax

Wakefield

Riding the Stang

Last night considerable stir and excitement prevailed at Northallerton consequent on the 'Riding the Stang'. The reason given in the doggerel rhyme which was repeated was that an ostler attached to a well known hostelry had proved unfaithful to his bride, whom he had married a short time ago. In a small pony cart an effigy was placed & the ringing of a bell, together with the shouts of those who were in attendance, created quite a hubbub. It is between three and four years since a similar exhibition took place.

(York Herald, March 1837.) Two days later:

Last night the final riding of the stang took place at Northallerton for the unfaithful ostler. The two figures were paraded round the town, after which a bonfire was lit on the green below the church, & after the doggerel rhyme had been proclaimed the figures were burnt.

There are several definitions of the old practice of Riding the Stang. Robinson, in his *Glossary of the Whitby Dialect*, lists it as "a public reproof to the husband or the wife notorious for quarrelling or going astray." The Oxford Dictionary calls it "a medley of sounds; a hubbub; a serenade of pans, trays etc. to an unpopular person." Somebody else called it a "jocular persecution". Sometimes it was not so jocular either.

There is no doubt that the custom is very old, probably pre-Christian in origin and can be connected to the Charivari in France, the punishment of Riding Skimmington in Hampshire and the Shivaree in early Canada. The word 'stang' comes directly from the Saxon 'stenge' - a pole, rod or stake. The word appears in most European languages in different forms. It was used for the pole of an ox-cart, the pole on which a butchered ox was hung and also in such forms as Stangend, a farm near Danby.

Although latterly it may have developed into a kind of frolic for the more unruly elements in a town, there is behind the custom a serious attempt to control the morals and behaviour of the community. It was a public protest and probably an effective one.

At Thirsk it was carried on well past the middle of the nineteenth century. A series of ridings there might occupy a week, each one having three ridings. The doggerel verses were changed every night by the leader of the stang band and he was, at the time, an important officer of the town. On the last night an effigy was burnt outside each offender's door. The leader would then knock on the door and ask for money; originally it was a groat but later much more would be necessary to satisfy the thirst of the band. There was a modified version in which the leader not the offender was carried on a ladder and later on a cart.

The magistrates would never interfere unless there was property damage. There are records of very satisfactory results following the rides, where the justices had quite failed to reform a wife-beater or a similar offender.

In Northallerton it was the culprit who was fastened to the pole and carried about the streets. Later he was represented by a straw effigy which was later burnt before his door. The procession was accompanied by the most horrible racket of banging pots and buckets and the chanting of an appropriate song :

"With a ran, tan, tan,
On my old tin can,
Mrs —— & her good man.
She banged him, she banged him
For spending a penny when he stood in need,
She up with a three-footed stool,
She struck so hard & she cut so deep
Till the blood ran down
Like a new-struck sheep."

Over the years, it seems the custom became stylised into two main forms. In one an effigy would be made of the offender of old clothes stuffed with straw and this was carried on the stang three nights running past his (or her) house. Sometimes a hand cart or a trap was used and there would be much shouting and banging of pots and pans. On the third night the effigy was burnt. Sometimes it was hanged first. Often a person was carried.

There are many records scattered about old documents and newspapers, as in Cramond in 1740: "Sundry riotous persons fin'd for carrying Ann Miln from her house and causing her to ride the stang." In 1777 Bourne's *Popular Antiquities* said that the word 'stang' was still used in some colleges in the University of Cambridge. To stang scholars at Christmas time

65

was to ride them on a colt-staff or pole for missing chapel. There are also records of what may be a debased form of stang-riding in which anyone caught by a gang of village rowdies out on New Year's Eve was made to pay a fine or ride the stang.

There seems to be little information about the variant used in Hampshire and other parts of southern England which was called Riding Skimmington. It seems largely to have been derisory of hen-pecked husbands and was a joint performance of a man and his wife riding together either on a horse or a pole. The man rode behind the woman carrying a distaff and the woman belaboured him with a frying pan, or sometimes carried a chemise like a banner. As there does not seem to be any etymological explanation for the word 'Skimmington' it may be a proper name, since lost, of some place or, perhaps, that of a notorious scold.

There is a rather curious case quoted by Richard Blakeborough of some person, unnamed, who when giving a lecture in Scarborough took it upon himself to accuse the Whitby lifeboatmen of being drunk in charge of their boat, which had recently been upset. The incensed Whitby lifeboatmen made an effigy of the gentleman, carried it down to the sands and burnt it there.

Then there is the notorious case of the unfortunate Parson Wikes of Leaseholme. His living included Ellerburn and, on arriving to conduct a service there one Sunday, he was horrified to find his whole congregation, including the clerk and the sexton, gathered in a cheering ring round a man and his wife having a violent quarrel on the opposite side of the beck. The combatants had reached a stage of considerable physical violence when Parson Wikes arrived. Disgusted by this behaviour on the Sabbath he leapt the beck and attempted to separate the pair amid shouts of encouragement to them and yells of "leave 'em be!" to the parson.

No doubt Parson Wikes was moved by the best of motives but was unaware that he was making a serious mistake in attempting to interfere in an argument between a man and his wife. There was a local custom, as in many other places, that he who meddled, even as a peacemaker, in such marital matters must ride the stang.

A pole was found and the unfortunate parson perched upon it. Usually the quarrelling man and wife were made to ride as well but these two belligerents were still busy combing each other's hair. The pole was raised onto some of the men's shoulders and an attempt was made to cross the beck with it. One of the bearers stumbled and this upset the whole equilibrium and the parson slid off into the water. Now wet to the skin Parson Wikes managed to arm himself with a stick and made a fighting retreat into the church.

In Europe the Charivari degenerated from its original usage and became associated with political lampoons and cartoons in such publications as the Paris *Charivari*, London's *Punch* and Berlin's *Kladderedatsch*. However, the Charivari did cross over to the New World and, in Canada, became the Shivaree and continued with typical stang riding punishments for social misbehaviour. Often there it would be directed against persons who were considered to have made a shameful marriage, especially where there was a great age difference between a man and his wife.

Susanna Moodie, in *Roughing it in the Bush*, tells of a case in Canada in the summer of 1833. She says: "I was startled one night just before retiring to rest, by the sudden firing of guns in our vicinity, accompanied by shouts and yells, the braying of horns, the beating of drums and the barking of dogs." A neighbour came in to tell her that "a set of wild fellows have met to shivaree Old Satan," who was another neighbour and had married his fourth wife that night, a young girl of sixteen. When the shivaree appeared at Old Satan's house, hooting and banging, he appeared at an upper window demanding to know what they wanted.

"We've come to drink the bride's health," shouted the leader. "Let us in."

"Can't do that nohow," was the reply. "How much to go away?"

"Thirty dollars," replied the leader.

"Can't do that neither," replied Old Satan. "Give you fifteen."

And, after a lengthy and good-natured argument, they settled for twenty and the crowd went away well pleased with itself.

In other cases things did not always turn out so peaceably. There were several fatalities and injuries. One of these was a negro who had married a white girl. He was made to ride the pole and beaten so badly that he died. In another case an outraged husband fired a charge of buckshot into the crowd and seriously wounded two of the men. This, of course, did not add to the man's popularity in the town and he eventually had to sell up and move elsewhere.

Like many other similar folk remedies, such as the Scold's Bridle and the Ducking Stool, the Charivari and the Stang have not survived the onset of urbanisation and more efficient policing. It would be difficult to argue, however, that any of our present communities, large or small, are better managed by modern methods - if there are any - of discouraging the types of social misbehaviour which were the province of the Charivari, the Stang and the Shivaree.

Money, Food and Sticks

There are two old Yorkshire folk tales which are so similar in plot that they must have come from the same original source and have been varied by different storytellers over the years. This is an interesting case of how, even in such a limited area as Yorkshire, such tales can develop along different lines in the different ridings. The first is, I believe, that told in the East Riding and the second in the West. I have never heard of a North Riding variant but there may well have been one. They are not told here in dialect.

The Woodcutter and his Three Sons

Once long ago there was a poor woodcutter who had three sons. They lived and worked in the forest, the father cutting the wood and the sons making up the faggots. The eldest son determined that he would better himself and so set off to make his fortune. When he had travelled most of the day he sat down to rest on the slope of a hill. Being somewhat tired he dozed a while and then woke up with a start to find a little man no higher than his knee standing looking at him.

"Who are you?" asked the youth.

"A friend," replied the little man. "If you want a safe lodging for the night, go over the hill and you will come to a white house. Tell them Harry Cap sent you and they will take you in."

So the youth went over the hill and, sure enough, there was the white house. When he told the people of the house Harry Cap had sent him, they welcomed him in and put him to bed after giving him a good supper. In the morning they gave him a present of a purse which had and always would have one piece of money in it.

With his fortune thus made the youth set off for home. On the way he was benighted and went to a small inn by the wayside. Here he paid for his supper from the magic purse but unfortunately the innkeeper's daughter was a witch and she noticed the purse and realised its value. She told her mother to make another just like it and, in the night, she changed them, leaving the poor youth just a piece of money to pay his shot.

The next day the youth reached home and, calling all his neighbours to witness his good fortune, promised them a piece of money each from his magic purse. When the purse would not even produce one piece of money the neighbours loaded him with abuse and went away in high dudgeon.

His brother's unfortunate experience did not deter the second son from making his bid for fortune and away he went. As with his brother before him, Harry Cap sent him over the hill to the white house where he was as well received as his brother had been. This time the people of the white house gave him a table which would never fail to produce any quantity or kind of food which was asked for. As his brother the second son arrived at the inn carrying the table on his back and retired straight to his room without asking for any supper. There he had a sumptuous meal from his magic table. However the landlord's wicked daughter had seen through the keyhole what was happening and, as they had a very similar table stowed away in the attic, she was able to exchange them in the night.

And so the second brother arrived home with a now useless table. As his brother had done he called the neighbours, this time to feast from his table. When no food appeared the neighbours were so incensed at what they thought to be trickery that they beat him and cursed him and his brother roundly.

So the youngest son set out to make his way in the world. As his brothers had done he also met Harry Cap and was directed to the white house and was as kindly received as his brothers had been. In the morning they gave him a knobbly stick which, when told to beat anybody, would set about them and thrash them soundly. And he too put up at the same inn on his way home. The witch daughter had noticed the stick and, during the night, crept into the room to get it. Now the youngest son was a smart lad and he had realised how his brothers had been tricked. He was on the watch and as soon as the daughter touched the stick he cried, "Up and bang her."

The cudgel, as if possessed by the devil, began to beat her all round the room until she agreed to give him the stolen purse and the table.

This time when the youngest son came home the neighbours were royally fed from the table and each was given a piece of money from the purse. But, when all the feasting was over, the youngest son called for quiet.

"Neighbours," he said, "when my brothers returned from their journeys they could not entertain you as you expected. So, taking no heed of their goodwill towards you, you abused and beat them instead of sharing their sorrow."

Then, turning to the stick, he cried, "Up stick and bang them."

So out of the house and along the street and over the bridge the stick drove them, and black and blue the neighbours were the next morning.

The Ass, the Table and the Cudgel

Once there was a lad called Jack who was so misused at home by his father that he made up his mind to run away and seek his fortune. So away he went, running and running until he ran bang up against an old dame and she, being good-hearted, said that he seemed to be a likely lad and she would take him on as her servant and pay him well. This seemed a fairish start to the lad so he agreed and went with the old dame to her house in the wood.

He served her there for a year and a day. When the time was up the old dame took him to the stable and pointing to an old donkey said: "There's thy wages lad, and good wages too." And she showed him that when the donkey's ears were pulled it made him "hee, haw" and out of his moth poured a stream of sixpences, shillings and even guineas. You can be sure that Jack was pleased with his earnings and away he went for home riding the ass.

He stopped at a roadside inn and ordered the best room and the finest fare that was to be had.

"Oh no, my lad," said the landlord, "first I want to see the colour of your money."

So Jack went out to the stable and, by pulling the donkey's ears, soon had a pocketful of money. But the landlord was a sly one and he had followed and watched what Jack did through a crack in the door. When night fell the landlord exchanged an ass of his own for the magic donkey. Jack did not notice that a change had been made when he set off for home the following morning.

In the same village as Jack's father there lived a poor widow with her daughter. This lass and Jack had been sweethearts for many a day but Jack's father would not let them marry until Jack had the money to support her. When he arrived home Jack again asked his father's leave to marry the girl and got the same answer as before.

"But I have the money now," said Jack and, going to the donkey, pulled its ears until it brayed and brayed and the more he pulled the more it brayed, and the more no silver and gold came out of its mouth. In a rage at his son, Jack's father beat him out of the house.

In a panic Jack ran and ran until he banged into the door of a joiner's shop which burst open and let him in.

"What's up?" asked the joiner.

"I've run off from home," replied the panting Jack.

"Well," said the joiner, "you look a likely lad. Serve me for a twelvemonth and I'll pay you well."

So Jack served the joiner for a year and a day and at the end the joiner said that, for his wages, he would give him a table which would instantly be covered with food when the order "table, be covered," was given.

Off went Jack with the table on his back until he came to the same inn. Calling for the landlord, he asked for the best food the house could offer.

"Nay, we've nought but bacon and eggs," said the landlord.

"Bacon and eggs!" cried Jack. "I can do better nor that. Come, table, be covered."

In that instant the table was spread with a cloth and on it turkey, duck, roast beef, fowl, mutton and all the vegetables you could think of. The landlord said nothing but, in the night, changed the table for one he had just like it in the attic. And the next morning, not knowing about this, Jack set off for home with the table on his back. When he arrived he went to his father.

"Now father," says he, "I have a plentiful store of food to offer a wife. We need never want for anything." So saying

74

he ordered the table to be covered but all in vain. Again his father, in a great rage, beat him out of the house.

Jack ran and ran, bawling miserably, through the forest till he came to a river and, before he could stop himself, had fallen in. A man ran up and pulled him out before he had come to much harm. The man asked Jack to help him build a bridge over the river. Jack agreed to this and was told to climb up to the top of a tree and lean out over the river so that, when the man chopped it down, it fell over the water and made a bridge over which the man could cross. The man thanked Jack and for his wages cut and shaped a branch from the tree into a useful club.

"Now then," says the man, "take this stick and if you say to it 'Up stick and fell 'em' it will beat anyone who injures you."

Now Jack was not nearly so daft as he seemed and knew now that the landlord at the inn had tricked him. Back he went to the inn. As soon as the landlord appeared Jack said, "Up stick and fell him." The cudgel flew straight from his hand and beat the landlord black and blue until he yelled for mercy. However, Jack would not tell the stick to let up until he had made sure of his donkey and his table. Then he trotted away for home on the ass with his table on his back and his cudgel in his hand.

At home he was greeted by the news that his father had died in his absence at which, perhaps, he should have shown more sorrow than he did. However, he put the donkey in the stable and pulled its ears until the manger was full and overflowing with money. He gathered it all up and took it into the house.

The village folk soon understood that Jack had come home with more money than he rightly knew what to do with. He made it known that he would marry the richest lass in the village and that, tomorrow, all the lasses were to come to his door with all their money in their aprons.

So all the lasses came with their aprons full with what money they had. Of course Jack's sweetheart was among them but she being very poor had only two copper pennies in her apron.

"Come over here, lass," Jack says to her, "there's nowt much in thy apron so stand over there."

She did as she was bid but the sad tears ran down her cheeks, ran into her apron and filled it with diamonds.

"Now up stick and fell 'em," cried Jack. And, at these words, the cudgel leaped from Jack's hand and knocked down every one of the other lasses into the roadway. Only Jack's sweetheart was left standing aside. Then Jack took all their money and poured it into her apron.

"Now thee art the richest," says he, "and I'll marry thee."

Hobs, Boggarts, Kobolds or Hobgoblins

My family and I were lucky enough to live for a while on a farm in a Yorkshire dale which, before its name was changed to Yew Grange, had been known for hundreds of years as Hob Garth. When we arrived there in the 1950s we would have loved to have taken the old name back but a neighbour had purloined Hob Garth for his reconstructed old cottage nearby. Unfortunately the hob, as well as the old name, was long gone.

There was another farm further down the dale which had also once had a hob and there were still old folk in the Dales who could remember some of the old tales about hobs and the nightime work they did to help the farmers who were lucky enough to have such an assistant.

It is perhaps not surprising that there are no reliable sight records or descriptions of the many hobs which were once doing their thing all over Yorkshire and beyond. There was a famous one in Farndale, at least two in Glaisdale and others at Castleton, Danby and, curiously, one in a cave near Runswick Bay who was some kind of witch doctor or healer. He was believed to cure whooping cough and other childish ailments. Whether the mothers who took their whooping offspring to the hob's cave saw him is not told, but the chant for assistance to the hob has survived:

> "Hob-hole Hob
> My bairn's gotten t'kin cough
> Tak't off, tak't off."

It has been suggested that hobs were perhaps relics of the Picts struggling to survive in a strange world, or brownies, or dwarfs, or boggarts - who knows? They have been variously described as short, brown and ugly or dwarf-like and wearing 'Hardin Hamp' - the farm labourer's smock with a hood. Like elves and fairies they were tricksy and easily angered or upset, when they would leave the farm and never come back.

Way back in the reign of the first Elizabeth, the famous Reginald Scot describes how boggarts and hobgoblins were looked after by the maidservants in the houses where one of these creatures lived.

"Indeed your Grandam's maids were wont to set a bowl of milk before him and his cousin Robin Goodfellow, for grinding the malt or mustard, and sweeping the house out at midnight, and you have also heard that he would chafe exceedingly if the maid or good wife of the house, having compassion on his nakedness, laid clothes for him beside his mess of white bread and milk, which was his standing fee, for in that case he saith: 'What have we here? Hemten, hamten, here will I never more tread or stampen.' "

There is one local instance, typical of several, where a farmer, and his father and grandfather before him, had carried on the common practice of leaving each night a bowl of cream for the hob who was believed to be friendly and helpful with such things as his nightime flailing the grain on the granary floor. The farmer, however, was misfortunate to remarry after the death of his first wife, and the second mistress of the house was of a mean and saving nature and she decided to save on the cream supplied to the hob by substituting milk instead. The hob spilt the milk and broke the bowl and was never heard of again.

Then there is the apocryphal tale of the farmer who was so bothered and driven to despair by the noisy, boisterous behaviour of a hob that he decided the only thing to do was to move elsewhere. In this case there seems to have been evidence of poltergeist activity - stone throwing, the pulling off of bedclothes etc., which probably stemmed from one of his children. So he packed up all the family belongings into the farm cart and set out to move to another farm.

Going down the dale he met a friend who asked:

"Where's ta goin', George?"

The farmer replied: "We're flittin' - t'owd hob's gotten t' better on us."

"Aye, we're flittin'," said a coarse voice from the back of the cart. It was the hob.

"Dang ye," shouted the farmer. "It thoo's coming we maun as well be off back agin!" And they turned round and went back.

It seems that what truth there is in these tales must be related to old stories of giants, dwarfs, fairies and True Thomas and their origins are lost in a past too distant for recovery.

Captain Stonehouse
and the French Privateer

Captain Christopher Stonehouse was a native of Yarm.
He was born in 1763 and went to sea as a youth in the coal
trade from Newcastle, and then in the wine trade with Portugal.

In his late thirties he was in command of the *Jenny* and
was part of a convoy of about fifty which set sail on a course
for home from Portugal. The convoy was under the protection
of H.M. Sloop of war *La Poulette* of twenty guns.

In the Bay of Biscay they ran into heavy weather and
the *Jenny* lost the convoy and was sailing on her own when,
about three days later, a cruiser was sighted at some distance.

It turned out to be a French privateer, a brig of eighteen
guns with a large crew.

The Frenchman soon came up with the *Jenny*, ran close
under her stern and, hailing her captain, ordered him to tack
to windward.

This he refused to do until compelled by heavy gunfire
from the enemy. He ran about two miles to westward and was

81

ordered to lay to. A large boat was hoisted out from the privateer with the intention of taking possession of the prize.

Several times Captain Stonehouse set sail and ran. He had a crew of only eight, two of them Italians and they refused to give the Captain further assistance because, they said, doing so would only lead to being subjected to harsher treatment later. Now Captain Stonehouse could see that the privateer was coming up with him again. He ordered the crew below and took the helm himself. The privateer raked the *Jenny* with heavy fire in passing without doing much damage. From her great speed in passing she ran considerably ahead of the *Jenny*, her boat towing astern of her. Captain Stonehouse decided to try to cut her boat adrift by sailing astern of the Frenchman. Instead he rammed her a little abaft of her main rigging, carrying away the main boom. The *Jenny* struck her so violently on her quarter that the whole ship and crew were thrown into great confusion.

Damage to the English ship was fortunately slight and was later described as "quite trifling". When the captain saw the crippled and confused state of the enemy he called up his crew and made all sail possible. In less than an hour and a half the privateer was out of sight.

He had to fight more gales which did further damage to the ship on the way home but arrived in Portsmouth on December 13th. The Underwriters at Lloyds, as a mark of approbation and reward, granted him two per cent of the cargo - presumably wine - valued at 14,000 pounds. He was later made a freeman of Newcastle.

He retired to Yarm but later moved to Stranton where he died in 1840, a local hero.

Baccy for the Clerk

For reasons not very far to seek the smuggler has always been looked upon with an indulgent eye by the average Yorkshireman. This, despite the opinion, doubtless with his tongue in his cheek, of the writer of a tract published in Stokesley in 1806 that says "it is doubtless a greater sin to cheat the government than to cheat a private person".

From the mid-eighteenth century until well into the nineteenth there can be no doubt that great quantities of taxable goods such as wines, spirits and tobacco were smuggled into the Yorkshire coast. Apart from the obvious dangers to unwary seamen, the rugged coast between Flamborough and Saltburn must have been a nearly ideal landing place for the smugglers. The wild country behind gave every opportunity for rapid dispersal of the runs through a well organised system of helpers and sympathisers.

In the Whitby district there are many tales of stow-holes, secret cellars, cavities in walls and so on. Near the Mulgrave Castle Inn, which once stood above Upgang a mile or so up the coast from Whitby, there were reported to be large caves behind a retaining wall which could be got at by taking out the stones from the wall itself. In 1817 more than two hundred tubs of gin were seized at this place.

The "hidy-hole" is supposed to have been discovered by a young stonemason named Adam Hewitt. The Preventives had got wind of a heavy run having been landed at Upgang and set off, accompanied by an interested crowd, to investigate. Hewitt appears to have been helping the authorities. At any rate, he noticed that a stone in the wall near the lime-kilns did not seem to have been set properly and, when the stone was pulled out, the cavity was discovered. A very large quantity of goods was brought out and carried in carts back to the Custom House in Whitby amid much jeering and shouting from the mob. It is said that when the men were unloading their haul at the Custom House, one of the kegs slipped and smashed into the kennel. Some of the watching crowd lay down and tried to lap up the spilled spirits. It is also reported that several casks mysteriously disappeared and that a real orgy was had in the fields between Whitby and Upgang.

However, the Preventives were not quite as clever as they had thought themselves for, the following morning, it was found that they had missed another hiding place nearby. The hole was, by then, emptied but the smugglers had left a note saying: "Look here and weep, three hundred tubs went from here last night."

The inn and all its secrets collapsed in rubble and fell over the cliffs years ago, but I can remember parts of it still standing when I was a youth, and there are pictures of it by George Weatherill and others.

The Ship Inn at Saltburn was another noted smugglers' haunt. The alert for the imminent arrival of a run among the local fraternity was the sentence: "Andra's coo's calved."

Hornsea Church crypt was another place used as a store for run goods. One night when the clerk was in the crypt sorting the goods a terrible gale blew up which took off the church roof and felled the tower. The clerk had a seizure and ever afterwards thought that the storm was an act of God to punish him for his wickedness. This was in 1732.

On the cliff tops at Buckton there stands a large house which was built, so the story runs, by a retired gentleman from India. It is now a farmhouse. It was from here that a well organised route for smuggled goods was operated. The occupants of the house at the time cleverly circulated the rumour in the district that the imbecile son of a duke was incarcerated there. This imaginary imbecile was said to be so violent that he had to be kept in chains and watched day and night.

It was a good story and no strangers were allowed into the house for years except for a shipwrecked sailor, the sole survivor of the crew of a whaler which came ashore on the rocks below. He had managed to climb the cliffs and struggled half-dead to the door. He was taken in and nursed back to life. Later he would tell how, as he lay weak from fever, he often heard the clanking of chains and heavy footsteps in the attic overhead.

Much later, when smuggling had all but ceased on the coast, a passage was found at the cliff foot which appeared to lead directly towards the house above. A barrel of spirits was found lodged in it and, when it was moved, it could be seen that a roof fall had blocked the passage completely. Later still it was found that the house had very large cellars and a large attic with a lift shaft running between the two. No doubt contraband could have been brought to the house through the passage and stored in the cellars and attic without much fear of detection. Perhaps the noises heard by the sick sailor were the clanking of the lift chains and the tramping about of the smugglers.

One of the easiest and most profitable forms of smuggling was carried out for many years by the owners of fishing smacks and cobles. They would put to sea, ostensibly for a day's fishing, but would meet instead with French or Dutch luggers outside the territorial limit and there would be a transfer of cargoes to the satisfaction of both parties.

There is a story of one of the Staithes boats coming into Whitby harbour for repairs from which over a hundred tubs were safely landed, almost under the noses of the Preventive men. And there are tales of even more elaborate tricks which the Gentlemen got up to.

One evening a small vessel sailed slowly into Bridlington Bay, her canvas half furled, her flag at half mast and her crew standing bare-headed on deck. The Preventives probably had an eye on her, being automatically suspicious of any vessels arriving off the coast at that time of day. However, their suspicions were lulled when boats put off from the shop with the whole crew and a coffin. They landed and six of the crew shouldered the coffin and marched through the town in the twilight. Somehow the coffin never reached the churchyard but it, or its contents, were well on their way to York by the time the sailors returned to their ship, hoisted sail and rapidly disappeared into the night. The coffin was said to have been tightly packed with tobacco. It was much later when the Preventives, unable to locate a burial in any church in the town, realised that they had been tricked. So far as is known they never got their hands on any of the tobacco.

Things did not always go so well for the smugglers. There was a most indefatigable Prevention Officer, a lieutenant King, stationed at Whitby who, with his crew, was fortunate enough to capture a small cutter, the *Goede Hoop* of Ostend, on May 9th 1828. He took her within the limit and soon found that he had a rich prize. When the cargo was landed at the Custom House it consisted of 160 half-ankers of Geneva, 40 of spirits of Geneva, 114 of brandy, one chest and two casks of tea, 65 casks of Shag tobacco, 10 casks of Twist tobacco and 10 chests of snuff. The unfortunate smugglers, eight of them, all Dutchmen, were examined before the Justices at Whitby and were fined £100 each. Unable to pay the fines they were committed to York prison.

In the early part of the nineteenth century the Lords Commissioners of H.M. Treasury were responsible for the Customs and Preventive Service, and their officers began to hit the smuggling fraternity where it really hurt. Information about new hiding places aboard ships was passed around as they were discovered. Spies were at work in the Continental ports discovering the cargoes and the times of sailing of ships suspected of being bound on smuggling trips.

The following extracts from the Saltburn Customs Order Book of 1817 and onward give some idea of the kind of tricks Preventives were being faced with. It will be seen that they were well able to profit by their own internal information services.

A letter dated 2nd June 1820: *"Sir, three boats have been seized at one of the outports for having prohibited goods concealed in the following manner. The spare foremast and outrigger of each boat had been hollowed out from head to foot, goods had been introduced into the cavities and both ends neatly plugged and painted. I have to desire you will acquaint the different officers under your inspection therewith, and direct them to be vigilant in endeavouring to detect similar frauds.."*

September 29th 1820: *"Memo: Tobacco having been lately smuggled into one of the outports in a vessel's hawser in the following manner viz: The tobacco made up into a rope of two strands and then a hawser of three strands laid over it so that it could not be discovered without cutting or unlaying the rope. I desire that you be vigilant to detect such frauds."*

January 22nd 1821: *"Memo: A seizure of a fishing boat with seventeen cases of tobacco concealed under her lining having recently been made by an officer of the coast blockade off Sandgate, which goods were not discovered until the nets, ballast and bulkheads were removed and the linings ripped up. The above for your information and guidance."*

The Order Book has many other memos and letters describing hiding places and warning officers of ships with contraband having sailed or which were about to sail from foreign ports. Among other hiding places described was that on a fishing smack, *Flower of Glory*, Wm. Head, master. She had a false bow with a square removable panel held by screws, the heads of which were concealed by wooden bungs imitating freenails. The extra cavity would hold forty or fifty ankers of spirits. An anker was about eight and a half gallons. Four other boats were named as having been modified in such a way.

A smack, the *Good Intent* of London, John Brown, master, had an ingenious method of transporting a raft of tubs. She had a lead pipe fitted just abaft the fore scuttle which ran right out through the bottom of the hull. A rope to fasten to the raft of tubs was passed through the pipe and the tubs hauled up close under the hull. The top of the pipe, when not in use, was concealed by a small lead plate which, when tarred and pitched, "could scarcely be perceived".

The usual procedure when foreigners were caught smuggling was to fine them one hundred pounds each and this penalty or more was applied to landsmen, with prison if they could not pay. Fishermen or seamen were not so fortunate, as they were usually handed over to the Press Gang, when it was operating, and the capturer made a nice profit of twenty pounds apiece. There is an entry in the Order Book for the 30th of July 1825 giving the description of Stephen Church, a smuggler, taken by HMS *Brazen* and subsequently impressed aboard HMS *Victory*.

But all did not always go smoothly within the services. The turnover in boat crewmen, according to the Order Book, was quite high. Between eight and ten a year are recorded as being dismissed the Service for drunkenness and other offences. There were of course informers. One such man was William Mead of Burniston.

One of Mead's victims was James Law of Staintondale who, upon information being laid, was convicted and fined 700 pounds. He did not, or could not, pay this heavy fine and he lay in York Castle for fifteen months. After this time he was released although he still had not paid the fine. Had it been paid, Mead would have received half which, no doubt, accounts for his zeal in having James Law convicted again some months later. This time the fine was £350. Still unable to pay, Law stood trial once at York and twice in London. Fortunately for him one of the Crown witnesses died and the case had to be dismissed. So, once again, Mead did not get his blood money; more than that, he was charged with perjury.

While Mead was out on bail, Law had been in Scarborough on business with a friend and they were returning homeward late one night through Burniston. The two seem to have been somewhat merry for they stopped outside Mead's house and sang an untuneful and very unflattering song about Law's persecutor. There was a smash of glass as a window was broken from inside the house, a shot and Law fell fatally wounded.

The trial caused a considerable stir at the time, but Mead was only found guilty of manslaughter and imprisoned. He cannot have been in prison very long for only a few years later he was convicted of cattle stealing and transported.

One of the more usual devices for the concealment of goods in houses was a trapdoor under the floor, usually covered by a flagstone.

After a report of a run into Robin Hood's Bay had reached the Whitby Preventives, the order was given to search every house in the village. It is not recorded that they found anything but, in one cottage, an old woman sat in her chair in the middle of the room while a young girl swept the floor around her. Not wishing to disturb the old lady, the officer had a cursory look round and left. The old lady had been sitting on the trap-hatch beneath which lay a store of half ankers of Geneva.

Similar hiding places were made in fields and particularly in gateways, where a large stone could be laid over and covered with mud and cattle footprints. One of the ways in which spirits were distributed about the countryside was in bladders which the women hung underneath their voluminous clothing. There are stories of falls and the "bursting" of bladders to the discomfort of the carrier.

Robin Hood's Bay was, at one time, smuggling-minded almost to a man. Once, a well known smuggler, known locally as Leather Thumb, arrived off the Bay and sent word that he had a run ready to be delivered. The messenger returned with the news that the men dared not come out of their houses because the Press Gang was in town. Leather Thumb was not going to have his plans upset by a detail like this and landed the boat's crew to attend to the matter. The smugglers stormed the Rendezvous House where the Press Gang were and beat them up so severely that they fled, leaving, so the report says: "Many of their number in the ditches by the wayside, lame and helpless."

Robin Hood's Bay

Some of the smuggling vessels were quite well armed and several battles took place at sea. In July of 1777 the frigate *Pelican* came across a schooner out of Flushing in Bridlington Bay. She carried sixteen cannons and twenty swivels - quite a formidable armament. The *Pelican* gave chase but lost her in the night. Two cutters picked her up the following morning and gave chase, firing their bow chase guns, the smuggler replying with her stern chasers. The *Pelican*, hearing the firing, came up with them and took over the battle. It did not last very long however, as the *Pelican* would have eventually sunk the schooner which struck and was taken into Hull. Her cargo was found to be 7,728 gallons of Geneva, 3,540 pounds of tea and 107 pounds of coffee. She had about fifty men aboard, some of them wounded in the engagement.

Sometimes the smugglers staged reprisals to recover goods which had been confiscated. On October 6th 1779 three Excise Officers from Whitby descended upon an innkeeper in Robin Hood's Bay and seized some 200 casks of brandy and Geneva, 150 bags of tea and also a chest containing blunderbusses and cartouche boxes for twenty men. The Officers did not keep their booty for very long as a smuggler's crew commanded by a well known character called Dover rescued all but about 20 casks and bags of tea. Dover had, a little time before, carried out a similar raid on the Custom House at Hartlepool.

Exciting times! Well, perhaps, but I would not have cared to take the risk of being impressed into one of the Navy's floating hells.

North Country Riddles

The King of Northumberland sent the Queen of Northumberland a bottomless vessel to put flesh, blood and bone in.

> A ring.

Hippi-pippi sat atop t'wall, Hippi-pippi cannot fall, not a lady in the land can take Hippi-pippi by the hand?

> The sun

Wick at beath ends, deead int' middle?

> A plough.

There was a man rode through the sun, Grey Grizzle was his name, his saddle bow was gilt with gold, three times I've told his name.

> Was.

A little house, all in it good?

A nut.

Two legs sat atop o' three legs, one leg laid by. In comes four legs, snatches up one leg. Up gets two legs, throws three legs at four legs, and gets back one leg?

Man, stool, leg of mutton, dog.

Hicklety-picklety at one side t'wall, Hicklety-picklety at t'other. If you go near Hicklety-picklety, Hicklety-picklety will bite you all?

A nettle.

What goes upstairs on its head?

A shoe nail.

As round as a cup and all t'watter in t'world wouldna fill it up?

A sieve.

A house full, a hole full and you canna catch a bowl full?

Fog or smoke.

I went to t'wood and I got it. When I had it I looked for it. The more I looked the less I liked it. I brought it home because I couldn't find it?

A spell or thorn.

The Affair of the Feuding Smuggler

One tends to think of the old days on the Yorkshire Moors as being a time of quiet and peaceful pursuits. If times were hard for the poorer folk, most of the Dales were pretty quiet backwaters. However, early in the nineteenth century the folk in Danby Dale in Cleveland had an uneasy few months when a seaman began a personal vendetta against one of the farmers in the Dale.

It was about the year 1807. Danby Dale at that time had a number of Quaker families among its farming community and one of these, that of George Baker, lived at Honey Bee Nest. Baker, in addition to running his farm, had recently been elected Parish Overseer. When he came to look over the books to see who was drawing relief he found that a woman from another parish had been allowed to draw relief to which she was certainly not entitled. Naturally enough he stopped payment of this money and this was the source of all the trouble.

The woman had a son, a rough, unruly character who sometimes sailed as crew to the Greenland whale fishery and between whiles occupied himself with smuggling goods into the conveniently rugged Cleveland coast. He took immediate exception to what he considered to be this ill-treatment of his mother. He was heard, in more than one of the inns he visited, to threaten to kill George Baker. Nobody, least of all George Baker, took much notice of these threats but it seems the idea of a vendetta had taken hold of the man's not too bright mind.

The first sign of trouble came when a neighbour of the Bakers, William Hartas of Nook House, felt unwell one evening. He sent his maidservant, accompanied by a dog, over to Honey Bee Nest to ask for some medicine. On her way over she became alarmed by the behaviour of the dog which acted as if someone was following her. George Baker's man, John, who was courting her at the time, saw her back to Nook House taking one of the farm dogs with him. He was away so long that the Bakers went to bed leaving the back door unfastened for him.

A girl, who was on a visit to the Bakers, had left something in the kitchen and, on coming down to fetch it, was startled to hear someone moving in the passage to the back door.

"John, is it thee?" she called out, and on getting no answer rushed to the door and bolted it. Then she ran upstairs and told the Bakers. George Baker came down and after a short while John's voice was heard at the front of the house calling, "Master, let me in and put out the lights, there's rogues about."

John told how, when he had got back close to the house, the dog had become unusually upset. Then he heard clattering and banging from the stables and saw that there was a light in there.

96

Master and man sat up for the rest of the night. The noises continued for some time as if someone was looking for an implement to use to break into the house. However, no attempt to do so was made during the rest of that night.

When day finally came, steps were taken to strengthen the window fastenings and John was sent to the village to order shutters. While he was there he was told that the smuggler had been heard to threaten to "do for George Baker" for stopping his mother's allowance.

For about two months this rather bungling vendetta went on. Attempts were made about twice a week to break into the house and for all this time watches had to be kept. The great fear, of course, was of fire, for the roof was thatched and dangerously inflammable. It was fortunate that, despite the smuggler's mother having been heard to say, "The place ought to be burnt and an end made of it," the smuggler does not seem to have attempted to start a fire.

However, things did take a more serious turn one night. George Baker was taking his turn watching, sitting as usual on the seat in the chimney corner. For some reason he moved over to the other side. A moment later there was a crash of glass and a whaler's harpoon came hurtling through the window and thudded into the woodwork above where he had been sitting. A harpoon is not a very pleasant weapon to encounter and this very much upset the family.

Mrs. Baker maintained, as she did all through the affair, that her husband was under the eye of God and, for that reason, had been impelled to move just before the arrival of the deadly harpoon. Nevertheless she, like the rest of the household, was under considerable stress which was only increased by this latest outrage. No doubt their persecutor was aware of the Quaker attitude towards violence and took full advantage of it.

Shortly after this came the time for a parish meeting and George Baker had all the books ready for audit when, on the night of the meeting, he felt so unwell that he did not go himself but sent his man John with the books and his apologies.

It was dark when John returned up the dale. He had to pass through a small plantation where the road dips down to a stream and then suddenly rises again, so slowing the pace of a horse considerably. It was here that the smuggler, presumably with a confederate, must have planned to waylay George Baker. As he climbed the rise John heard a voice say, "Stop, this ain't him." We may be sure that John made all haste to get away from that unhealthy spot.

This experience increased the anxiety of the Bakers and their friends. Neighbours helped by taking turns at watching and, after several weeks of this, tempers, not unnaturally, began to wear a little thin.

Several times the smuggler partly forced the pantry window. They tried to trap him by various means without success. An attempt was made to persuade George Baker to allow the use of firearms but to this he would not agree. In the end it was John who decided that he had had enough. Hearing the smuggler again at the pantry window, he took down a gun that he had previously prepared and fired through the window. Perhaps, fortunately for everyone, he did not kill the man. The following morning a bloody imprint of a hand was found on the gate, so it was known that the smuggler had been injured.

A reward was put up for the arrest of the injured smuggler but he managed to evade capture and disappeared for a while. It was said that he had his wound dressed by an "irregular practitioner" at Stokesley who must, presumably, have had his palm well greased to prevent him going to the authorities and claiming the reward.

The final peculiar conclusion came a few weeks later. Sarah Baker, George's wife, was at home with her two small children and the maidservant. The men were some distance away in the fields. To her astonishment and terror the smuggler suddenly appeared in the doorway. He had his hand bandaged and his arm in a sling.

"A've cum ti see George Baker an' ti gie micel up," he said and then added, "an' ti claim t'reward."

For a moment Mrs. Baker wondered whether to bang the door in his face but, with a great show of calmness, she invited him in and gave him a meal. The maidservant quietly slipped out to warn George Baker to keep out of the way until the dangerous visitor had gone.

As it happened help was not far away. Two of the neighbours, George Hartas and John Baker, had seen the smuggler coming up the dale and followed him. They were now at the front of the house ready to rush in at the least sign of trouble. Mrs. Baker must have been greatly reassured by the glimpse she had of them through one of the windows. Her one fear was that her husband might come in before she had got the smuggler out of the house.

It was soon dusk and George Baker had not returned so George Hartas went into the house and said, "Now Harry, thou knows thy character is not good, it would beseem thee to be going home," and to the great relief of everybody he went and, as far as is known, never returned.

Rumour had it that he became a reformed character and developed into a local preacher but this seems unlikely. It would seem more likely that the Press Gang at Whitby got him or that he was lost on a whaling trip.

Yorkshire

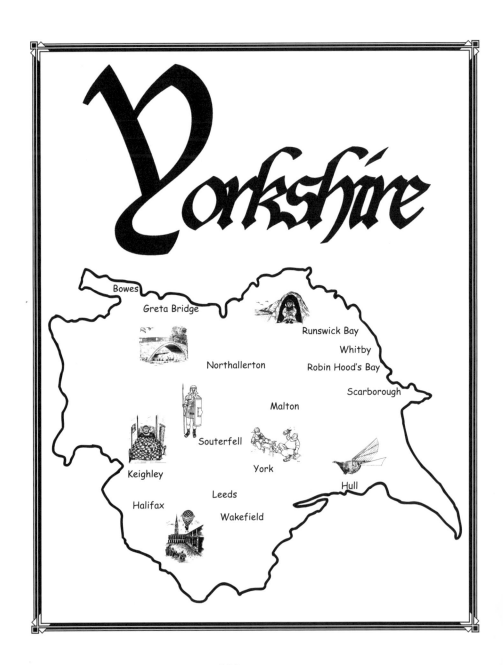

Bowes

Greta Bridge

Runswick Bay

Whitby

Northallerton

Robin Hood's Bay

Scarborough

Malton

Souterfell

Keighley

York

Hull

Leeds

Halifax

Wakefield

Phantom Troops and other Marvels

One Sunday evening in the June of 1912 Anthony Jackson and the son of a neighbouring farmer were looking round some cattle on the Jackson farm near Harrogate. As they walked through the fields they were suddenly astounded to see, marching along at some distance from them, a large body of troops in white uniforms. In the centre of the troop was a soldier in scarlet whom they described as being "of a commanding aspect".

The troop carried out several manoeuvres and then set off in perfect marching order towards the top of a nearby hill. They passed only about a hundred yards in front of the spellbound men and, four abreast as they were, they filled an enclosure of nearly thirty acres. Still marching steadily they passed over the top of the hill and a second troop, more numerous and dressed in black, appeared and marched after them. As the soldiers passed over the hill a thick pall of smoke was seen, but this soon cleared and no more was seen of them.

Another curious case occurred near Stockton-on-Forest on the 13th of January, 1792. This time the troops were seen in the sky. There were several separated divisions of what seemed to be a large army. Some of the men were dressed in white and some in black uniforms. One of the divisions formed a line which was thought to be nearly a mile long and among the men a number of fir trees could be seen. The trees seemed to move along with the troops. The various groups of soldiers moved about in different directions, sometimes with great rapidity.

Another account of a happening of this kind is given by James Clarke in his *Survey of the Lakes of Cumberland* published in 1789. The witnesses gave signed statements of what they had seen and the second of the occurrences was seen by at least twenty six people. According to Clarke's account this is what happened.

On a summer evening in 1743 when Daniel Strickett, servant to John Wren of Wilton Hall, was sitting at the door with his master, they saw a man with a dog pursuing some horses along Souterfell Side, a place so extremely steep that a horse could hardly travel along it at all. The figures appeared to run at an amazing pace until they passed out of sight at the lower end of the fell. On the following morning Strickett and Wren climbed up the steep fellside in the expectation of finding some traces of the passage of the man and horses. They said they expected to see cast horse shoes or even to find the man lying injured. Instead they found nothing, no disturbed or scraped stones nor a single hoofmark on the turf. At first, as is usual in these cases, they kept what they had seen to themselves and when, after some time, they told their story they were only laughed at for their incredulity.

On the 23rd of June of the following year Daniel Strickett, who was now servant to a Mr. Lancaster of Blakehills, a place near Wilton and also within easy sight of Souterfell, was walking near Wilton about seven in the evening a little above the house. This time it was a troop of horse soldiers that he saw riding on Souterfell Side in pretty close ranks at a good pace. Thinking of the ridicule that he and Mr. Wren had received the year before, he watched the figures for some time in silence. At last, being convinced that there could be no deception this time, he went to the house and told Mr. Lancaster that he had something to show him. Before Strickett could point out the figures, Mr. Lancaster's son had seen them. The rest of the family were then brought out.

The riders seemed to come from the lowest part of Souterfell and became visible at a place called Knott. They then came in regular troops along the side of the fell until opposite Blakehills. From there they took a curving path and went over the fell top. The horses went at a regular swift walk and, for some two hours until darkness, they continued to pass. Many troops were seen in succession and often the last but one in a troop would leave his position at the rear and gallop to the front.

It is very difficult to suggest an explanation for these phenomena. They do not seem to be comparable with desert mirages or the phantom ships and ice palaces seen off Greenland by Captain Scoresby. There is the possibility that Strickett was psychic and was able to project unconsciously what was so clearly seen by others.

There is another story of a rather different sort, current in Cleveland in my youth, of marching Roman soldiers having been seen on the Roman road near Rutmoor Beck. One of the farmhands from Stape had walked over to Egton Bridge for a convivial evening at the pub there. At closing time he set off over the moorland track by Wheeldale and Rutmoor Beck. This road, which was then a rough track, crosses Rutmoor

Beck at a place where the Roman road crosses it. One would have expected that by the time the man reached this place his blood alcohol would have dropped considerably and his head would have been cleared by the sharp night air of the high moors. It was a clear starlit night when he sat down to rest on the bank of Rutmoor Beck.

He would never admit to having dozed off but said that he was suddenly surprised, but not at all frightened, by the sight of a company of men marching down the opposite bank slope towards the beck. As they crossed and marched away along the line of the old road which was still covered with heather he realised that they were wearing what he called "them there Scotch kilts". When they had gone he got up and went on his way.

There are plenty of records of severe and dangerous thunderstorms in the old records of Yorkshire, but none that I have seen so peculiar as that which happened on October 12th in 1658, if it was a thunderstorm at all. The reports all come from Holderness, Hedon and the Hull area.

The day was very clear with a bright sun shining all the time, except for a short eclipse-like period over Hull. The performance began with three loud explosions "like three great pieces of ordinance or cannons discharged in the air, one after another, very terrible to hear, and followed immediately by a peal of muskets". This sound, as of muskets, lasted several minutes and was accompanied by a sound like the beating of drums, just as if two armies had engaged. The two observers, who had thought that the noise came from Hull, believed that it was in honour of the Sheriff as it was his riding day.

Then the sky began to grow dim, as it does during an eclipse of the sun, and they had the strange feeling that the earth was trembling and shaking under them. At the same time a great mist of smoke almost obscured Hull from their sight.

A retired major who was riding with a friend between Patrington and Ottringham was so convinced that there was a battle going on somewhere that he spurred to the top of a nearby hill hoping to get a sight of it.

The noise, whatever it was, must have been something much out of the ordinary. Many were so frightened that they left their work and ran home. Coal pickers on the shore rushed off leaving their bags and pickings behind them.

One possible clue, the shaking of the ground recorded by only two observers, might suggest an earthquake. The witnesses are all dead, so we shall never know.

Furious Driving 1864

Mr. Willoughby Green was very proud of his old horse, Jack Rossiter. In his younger days Jack had been a real goer, outpacing almost anything put against him in that part of Yorkshire, but now he was getting on and when a chap called Robson told Mr. Green that Jack was past his time and no good any more, and that his little mare could leave Jack standing in a decent trot, Mr. Green was in two minds whether to take him on or not.

This chap Robson was a persuasive sort and very full of himself. He jockeyed Jack's owner into a position where he could hardly refuse to put the thing to the test. So, for a fifty pound-a-side stake, a trotting match of fifty miles between Leeming Lane and Leeds was arranged. The two owners were driving their own tits and a start was made at noon on June 27th, 1864.

Robson, in view of Jack's reputation, wangled a start of 500 yards, and away they went. Green kept Jack well in hand, thinking of the long miles ahead, and did not seem unduly bothered as Robson's mare rapidly increased her lead to over a mile. He knew that Robson was pushing his mare too hard. In fact Robson was driving like a madman or, as one onlooker put it, "very rashly".

However, some of Green's friends, who were riding behind him, became alarmed at the distance Robson had drawn ahead. After a bit of an argument they persuaded Green to depart from the plan he had laid down to keep Jack going steadily until Robson's mare tired.

"Get on his tail," they urged, "or pass him and his mare will break all the sooner."

So Green gave Jack the rein and the old horse responded magnificently. He rapidly overhauled Robson and his mare, passing them between Boroughbridge and Wetherby.

When the two contestants arrived in Wetherby it could be seen that both horses were about done up. The effort had really taken it out of Jack and Robson's mare was terribly blown. Green had to nurse Jack all the rest of the way to Roundhay - the winner.

The case was not so good with Robson's mare. The poor beast struggled all the way to the neighbourhood of Scarcroft, from which place right to Leeds the roadsides were lined with waiting spectators. Here the mare fell several times. Her owner got her into a stable where she laid down and never got up again. She was dead within minutes.

There can be no doubt that it was the pace to which she had been put in the early part of the race which had killed her. Old Jack had covered the whole distance in three hours and fifty minutes.

Not unnaturally, there was a good deal of criticism of both Robson and Green and eventually proceedings were taken against them for furious driving.

The case was heard in the West Riding Court in Leeds on July 5th. Green was charged with furious driving and cruelly over-driving his horse. He was found guilty and fined five pounds and costs. He immediately paid up.

Robson was charged similarly, but public feeling was much more strongly against him. He, too, was found guilty and sentenced to one month's imprisonment with hard labour. He appealed and was granted bail. However, his council cannot have thought much of his chances on appeal, for he advised him to submit to his sentence and he did.

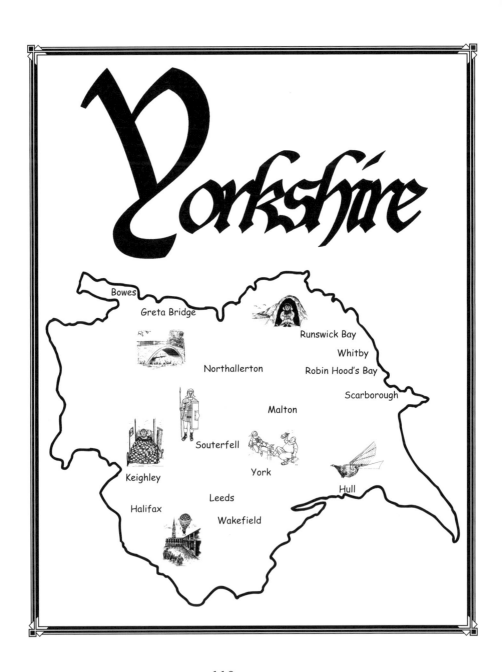

Yorkshire

Bowes

Greta Bridge

Runswick Bay

Whitby

Northallerton

Robin Hood's Bay

Scarborough

Malton

Souterfell

Keighley

York

Hull

Halifax

Leeds

Wakefield

Notes from the *Yorkshire Gazette* 1774

March 7th. The York and Newcastle Post Coach commenced to run, covering the distance in one day. Passengers from Newcastle breakfasted at Darlington, dined at Easingwold and reached The George in Coney Street, York at 6pm. Here they could reserve places in the London Fly which set off at 11pm.

The Newcastle first coach set off from the George at midnight, the passengers breakfasting at Northallerton, dining at Durham and arriving at Newcastle at six in the evening.

Six inside and two outside passengers were carried. The insides paid three guineas and the outsides 38 shillings and sixpence each from London to Newcastle. Those only travelling part of the way paid threepence a mile inside and twopence a mile outside. No liveried servant was taken inside without his master or mistress being with him. No children under two years of age were carried. Any proprietor allowing a dog to enter the coach was to be fined five pounds.

November 1774. The inhabitants of several of the parishes of York appointed proper persons to patrol the streets in the night time to preserve their persons and property from the depredations of these lawless freebooters infesting the neighbourhood.

December 18th. Thomas Knight of Tadcaster was coming over Rothwell Heigh when he was knocked down by a lusty man who stripped him of his clothing, shoes and buckles, then left him. He had only one shilling in his pocket.

A Yorkshire Gilpin:
The Parson's Ride to Malton

There was a certain Parson
Of fame and great renown,
Of Erin's Isle by birth was he,
Now rector of a sea-port town;
This Parson to his wardens said:
"Tomorrow's the Visitation,
And to the town of Malton
We'll have a nice excursion."

The morrow came - the wardens went
Direct unto the station,
Thinking that by train he meant
To go to the Visitation.
With tickets got and seats secured
They sat in expectation
Of seeing t'Rector rushing in
As t'train was set in motion.

The Churchwardens they began to stare
On hearing t'whistle tingle,
To think they should be left alone
In charge of Mr. Dingle.
Spurt went the steam, round went the wheels,
Folk were never more scared
At leaving behind their parson dear,
'Twas wonder they hadn't cried.

Just as the train the station left,
In came the parson fussing,
In time to see the carriages
Behind the engine rushing.
Then to an inn he did repair,
Yclept Angel and renouned
For best quality horseflesh there
Is always to be found.

The horse was brought, the girths were tied;
The Vicar always nimble,
Jump'd upon the prancing steed
Declaring he'd beat the D—gle.
Down came the whip on the horse's flank
To the hostler's sore amazement,
And prancing past the savings bank
He nearly came to t'pavement.

Baxtergate's soon left behind,
Also the Railway Station,
And soon at Ruswarp he arrives,
In a state of perspiration.
On his friend at the corner call'd
Made known his procrastination,
And left him in charge of his overcoat
Till his return from the Visitation.

The first stage of his journey won,
Procures for himself good feeding,
Resolved to change his distressed nag
For one of better breeding.
Now see him mounted once again
And getting into motion,
With good speed went he o'er the stones,
But with deuced little caution.

The horse who never in that way
Had handled been before,
What thing upon his back he'd got
Did wonder more and more.
But away went Parson, neck or nought,
To beat his wardens there,
Who little thought when they set out
Their feasting he would share.

At Malton town the dogs did bark,
Up flew the windows all,
And every soul cried out "well done!"
As loud as they could bawl.
Then off to church he bent his way
To attend the Visitation,
Overtook his wardens on their way,
Which caused a great sensation.

"I'll beat, I'll beat!" with all his might
Bawled the parson with delight,
Then into church he bolted straight
And so kept out of an awkward plight.
The Archdeacon gravely gave his charge,
Which one and all received;
They paid their money, signed their names,
And left the church for a feed.

Again he mounted on his nag
When it began to rear,
He whipped and spurred, then galloped off
As he had done before,
To beat the train to Pickering
He tried and did it soon,
Nor stopped till where he had got up,
He did it down again.

Now as the wardens homeward came
Behind the locomotive,
Their vicar with his whip in hand
Was at Pickering quite sportive.
At length they arrived at home again,
And told of the incumbent's work,
But the people all were inclined to think
The wardens were playing a joke.

For thirty miles the Parson kept
Good pace with the locomotive,
Surprised his flock, exercised his steed,
And accomplished his wonderful Motive.
Folk say, "The Parson's mad!"
But that we don't believe,
There's method in his madness,
And those who live will see.

Now let us sing, long live bold Ke—ne,
And D—gle, long live he,
And next when we to Malton go,
May they together be.

Broadsheet printed at Tommy Wilson's Steam Press, Malton.
Price one penny.

All for the Love of a Lady

William Sharp had a reputation for being tight-fisted. However that might have been, he was pretty well breeched, which for his son's sake was just as well. He was a farmer and a manufacturer of worsted and owned two farms. One, called Sheep Hole, or Two Laws as it was more usually called, on the Colne Road and Whorles, near Keighley, where he lived. He was said to have got his nickname, Old Three Laps, when he took a piece of cloth to a tailor to be made into a coat.

"Nay," said the tailor upon looking the piece over, "I mun have more cloth, this'll nobbut mak three laps."

"Then thoo mun make it wi three laps," said Sharp, and he went off. He soon found himself saddled with the nickname Old Three Laps. Being blessed with a son also called William, it was only natural that *he* should be known as Young Three Laps.

Young William grew up on his father's farms, working hard and living quite as any other young man. He spent much of his spare time hunting or drinking with his friends at the pub.

119

Until he was about thirty he doesn't seem to have shown much interest in women. Then he had the misfortune to fall in love.

The girl was Mary Smith of a nearby farm called Bottoms. Probably because young Bill had inherited some of his father's caution, the courtship was a lengthy one. However, they finally decided to marry. One report tells us that maybe a little stranger due to arrive at Bottoms had some voice in the matter.

The great day came and Bill arrived at the church dressed in his best but when, after a long wait, no bride appeared, Bill went to Bottoms to see what had happened. He found that the two fathers had disagreed about the monetary arrangements.

Mary's father said he wasn't going to give her a dowry unless Old Three Laps handsomely provided for his son. This Old Three Laps would not do, saying the young couple could live on the farm. So, after calling Old Three Laps a tight-fisted old devil, Mary's father refused to let her marry.

Bill took this hard. He went home, went to bed and stayed there until he died. His bedroom was nine feet by six feet. The last report we had of it was that it had been turned into farm buildings and was occupied by hens. When Bill was in solitary occupation it contained a bare four-poster without drapes, a small round table and a clock that did not work. The only ventilation was through the door. The small window was partly boarded up to discourage peepers. The floor was of stone flags and was damp. There was a small fireplace which smoked so badly that a fire could rarely be lit.

From his four-poster bed Bill flatly refused to move and there, seeing nobody but the attendant his father had hired for him and only rarely speaking, he stayed for thirty eight years. If any stranger came into the room he covered himself

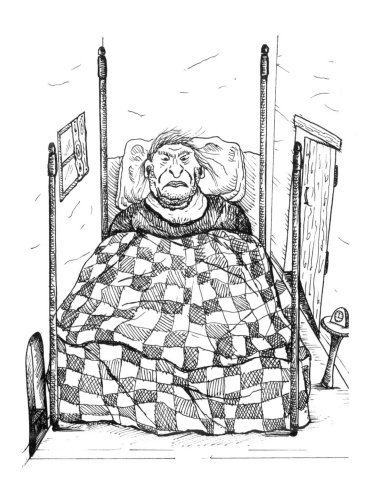

with the bedclothes until they had gone. In all that time he kept himself healthy and never suffered any illness.

When his father died Young Three Laps was left comfortably provided for and was able to carry on with his protest, which had by then become an entrenched habit. He always ate well and, over the years, put on a great deal of weight. His legs, through disuse and perhaps rheumatism, became contracted so that he could not stand or sit properly, but rolled himself into a kneeling position to eat his meals. He was always very fussy about getting any crumbs in his bed. He finally almost lost the power of speech and could only make inarticulate grunts.

On March 3rd, 1856 he died, speaking, just before he did so, the first coherent words for many a year: "Poor Bill - Poor Bill - Poor Bill Sharp." An unusual coffin, like a huge chest, had to be made because of his bulk and peculiar shape. It was assembled in the bedroom and then the window and part of the wall had to be taken away to get it out for the journey to the cemetery.

The weight of the coffin and Bill was said to be 480 pounds.

The Golden Ball

There were once two lasses, daughters of one mother, and as they came home from the fair they saw a beautiful young man standing in the house doorway. They had never seen anyone quite so magnificent before. He had gold in his cap, gold on his fingers, gold on his neck and a red-gold watch-chain. In each of his hands he had a golden ball. He gave one of the golden balls to each of the lasses and told them that they must keep them carefully, for if either lost her golden ball she would be hanged.

One day, some time later, the younger lass was playing with her ball, tossing it in the air, and it went higher and higher until it went over the palings. When she ran to look for it she saw it run along the green grass and go into a house door. She went after it but could find neither sight nor smell of it. It was lost and no mistake. Then they came and took her away to hang her because she had lost her golden ball.

Now this lass had a sweetheart and he said he would get her ball back and so save her. He went to the house where the ball had run and tried the gate. It was shut and locked so he could not go in that way. Then he climbed a hedge and, when he was on top of it, an old woman got up out of the ditch as he was about to jump down. She said if he would get the ball he must sleep three nights in the house. He said he would gladly do that and he went into the house and looked around but could find no sign of the golden ball.

Night came and he began to hear strange sounds from the courtyard. He went to a window and looked out and saw that the yard was as full of spirits as maggots in rotten meat. Then he heard steps coming up the stairs, so he hid behind the door as quiet as a mouse.

A great giant, five times as big as he was, came into the room. The giant looked round but missed seeing the lad and went to the window and bent down to look out. As he bent down with his elbows on the window sill to see the spirits in the yard the lad came up behind him and, with one blow of his sword, cut the giant clean in two. The top half of him fell out into the yard and the bottom half still stood at the window.

The spirits in the yard gave a great cry when they saw the top half of their master come tumbling from the window and they called out, "There comes half of our master, give us t'other half!" So the lad kicked out the bottom half of the giant and it fell among the spirits in the yard and they were quieted.

The second night the lad was in the house again and now another giant came tramping up the stairs. The lad let him get into the room and then sliced him in two with his good sword. But this time the legs went on walking and they walked straight on and up the chimney and vanished.

"Get after thy legs," says the lad and he threw the head half up the chimney and it went too.

124

On the third night no giant came so he got into bed and, while he was there, he heard spirits striving and struggling under the bed. They had the golden ball and were throwing it about under there. The lad waited till he saw a leg come out from under the bed, and then he brought his sword down "crack" and chopped it off. Then an arm came out on the other side and he chopped that off. So it went on until he had maimed them all and they went off crying and wailing and quite forgot the ball in their misery. So he took it from under the bed and went off to seek his true love.

Meanwhile they had taken the lass to York to be hanged. She was brought to the scaffold and the hangman told her to get ready as he was going to hang her by the neck until she was dead, but she cried out:

"Stop, stop, I think I see my mother coming.
Oh, hast thou got my golden ball,
And are you come to set me free?"

But her mother replied:

"I've neither got thy golden ball,
Nor come to set thee free,
But I have come to see thee hung
Upon the gallows tree."

So the hangman told her to say her prayers so that he could get on with his business. But she said:

"Stop, stop, I think I see my father coming.
Oh, father, hast thou got my golden ball,
And are come to set me free?"

And her father replied:

"I've neither got thy golden ball,
Nor come to set thee free,
But I have come to see thee hung
Upon this gallows tree."

Then the hangman asked her if she had said her prayers for she must put her head in the noose and be done.

But she went on saying, "Stop, stop!" because she thought she saw her brother and her sister, her uncle and her aunt and even her cousin coming to save her. Then the hangman quite lost patience and said he would stop for no more but would hang her forthwith. But now at last she saw her sweetheart forcing his way through the crowd holding his hand high above his head, and in it was the golden ball itself. So, once again, she called out:

"Stop, stop, I see my sweetheart coming.
Sweetheart, hast thou brought my golden ball
And are come to set me free?"

And the lad shouted his reply:

"Aye, I have brought thy golden ball,
And come to set thee free,
I have not come to see thee hung
Upon the gallows tree."

And he took the lass down from the scaffold and kissed her and gave her the golden ball. Soon after they were married and lived long and happy.

(This story, with its considerable psychological overtones, appears to have strayed into the north country from elsewhere. There was a well-known West Riding dialect version which I have not been able to locate.)

They Had Them in Those Days Too - Problem Child

Richard Clark was one of the notorious Faws Gang. This collection of scoundrels was largely made up of gypsies from the tribe in the border country which rampaged about the country in the mid-eighteenth century committing every sort of crime. It might be said that young Richard had the splendid example of his parents in developing his bad character. It all ended at York in 1767 when he was executed for breaking into a house at Knaresborough - one of his minor crimes.

Born at Spittall, near Berwick-on-Tweed, in 1739 he was, at the ripe age of eleven, thrown out into the world when his mother and father, together with William and John Fall and their wives, were ordered by the Quarter Sessions to be transported for seven years. They were taken from Morpeth Gaol, put aboard the *Owners Goodwill* and shipped off to South Carolina.

It would seem that transportation was not a very efficient way of getting rid of criminals - certainly not in the case of the Faws Gang. About a year later Richard, who had been getting along quite nicely by petty pilfering, was working Richmond Fair when he met one of his cousins who had just escaped from the Carolinas. It was not long before Richard's parents were back and busy plundering whatever they could from whoever they could.

They travelled much about the country and even put Richard to school at various places. Unfortunately his education was rather disturbed by his parents' sudden and frequent need to vanish for pastures new.

One of their expeditions took them to Ireland where the Clarks were imprisoned for theft but had, reluctantly, to be released for lack of evidence. It is more than probable that the other members of the gang had nobbled the witnesses.

About the year 1759 Richard, now a fully qualified scoundrel, was clapped up at Newcastle for highway robbery and was given his first taste of the New World. He was transported but in less than a year was back to the welcoming arms of his mother, father and the rest of the gang.

1762 saw him, now a married man, clapped up at Shrewsbury for horse stealing for which he received a sentence of death. They say the Devil looks after his own and, the day before his execution, he was reprieved and ordered to be transported to Maryland.

By this time he was an old hand at the transportation game and was soon back. During his absence his wife, who seems to have been a suitable partner, had been hanged at Coventry.

Richard, on his return, joined up with the gang at Newcastle and went back to work. Occasionally, when things became a little too hot for him, he would enlist as a soldier until the heat was off when he would desert and turn to the bosom of his deplorable mother and the rest of the gang. His father appears to have dropped out of the picture about this time. More probably he dropped with a rope round his neck and kicked his life away on the "nubbing cheat".

In 1765, Richard was convicted of house-breaking at Carlisle and was transported to Virginia. By this time he had travelled pretty widely in the colonies, but Virginia was no more successful in holding him than the others had been. Maybe he didn't find enough work suited to his talents, for he was soon on home ground again. Joining up with his mother they broke into several houses in the Newcastle area during the summer of 1766, but with little financial gain. They were more successful at a house near Durham where about 13 pounds went into the kitty.

Then at Knaresborough, in one Mark Hattersley's house, Richard met his Waterloo. He stole twenty four guineas but was taken. At York on April 18th, 1767, he was executed.

This time there was no return.

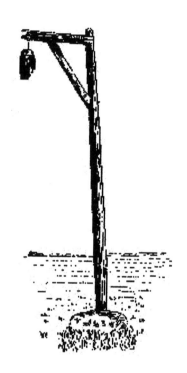

Problem Woman

An unhappy event for the north country took place in 1763 at Aisenby, near York. The wife of a small farmer presented him with a daughter.

From her earliest years Mary Harker was "addicted to petty pilfering and other villainous acts". In 1792, after a three week whirlwind courtship, she married John Bateman, an honest, hard-working man. He would have plenty of time to ponder on his impetuosity. The couple went to live in Leeds where Mary set herself up as a fortune-teller. She was clever enough to keep just out of the reach of the law but, nevertheless, succeeded in swindling her clients out of varying sums of money.

In 1796 there was a big fire in Leeds and Mary got the idea of going round collecting money and bedding for the benefit of the poor folk who had been made destitute by the fire. This was quite a successful operation but the only person who was to benefit was Mary Bateman.

About this time the Batemans moved to Black Dog Yard where Mary startled the neighbourhood with a miraculous egg on which was inscribed "CHRIST IS COMING". At this distance in time it is difficult to imagine how so many people came to part with a shilling for a sight of this marvellous egg.

In 1803 Mary got herself a job as assistant to two maiden lady drapers. The unfortunate ladies were suddenly taken ill and passed away, as did their mother who had come to nurse them. Mary passed the word round that they had died of the plague and the house was shunned for some time. This did not altogether stop the whispers that were going round that the ladies had been poisoned.

All this while Mary had been carrying on her fortune-telling business. One of her most profitable lines was the selling of charms to avert disasters which she herself had foretold.

A lady called Judith Cryer had a son who had got various minor sorts of trouble. Mary foretold that, unless she intervened, the lad would eventually be hanged. The frightened Mrs. Cryer pawned her bed and gave Mary four pounds to save him. Similarly with a Mrs. Snowden, whose offspring had been giving her cause for worry. From her Mary extracted twelve guineas and a silver watch. And she was not above playing minor tricks to obtain a good meal.

When she was in the Shambles one day, she overheard a gentleman order a leg of lamb to be delivered immediately to his house in Meadow Lane. She hurried to Leeds Bridge where she intercepted the butcher boy and, after giving him a good rating for being so long, said she would take the meat home herself. Which she did - to her own home.

Her unfortunate husband did not escape her plots. Finding herself rather short of the ready she forged a letter from Thirsk saying his father had been taken ill and was like to die. Her husband hurried off, hoping to see his father before the end. Of course, the puzzled man found his father quite well. But all was not quite so well when he returned home. He found that Mary had stripped the house of its contents and had sold the lot. Unfortunately, history does not report what her husband had to say about this.

Mary had had, until this time, a pretty good run and was not to know when she became involved with a small clothier called Perrigo in Bramley that she was, at last, going to have to answer for some of her crimes.

William Perrigo's wife was under the delusion that someone had put an evil wish on her. This, with the aid of an imaginary Miss Blythe, Mary set out to put right. In six months she had bled the Perrigos of seventy pounds and stripped their house of furniture and their best clothing. But still there was no cure. However, Mary thought one up.

She made up a honey pudding to which she added a certain charm. This noxious concoction certainly put Mrs. Perrigo out of her misery but Mr. Perrigo did not die, although his health was permanently affected. The death of his wife finally awakened Mr. Perrigo to the state of affairs and, as soon as he could stagger out, he went to a magistrate and laid the case before him. The result was that Mary was committed to York Prison. On the 17th of March 1809 she was convicted of the wilful murder of Rebecca Perrigo and sentenced to be executed on the following Monday. But Mary still had one trick up her sleeve - she told the judge that she was pregnant.

Under the law, if a convicted felon was found to be four and a half months or more pregnant, the execution must be delayed till after the birth. Unfortunately for Mary, the judge was a wily bird too, and immediately caused a jury of twelve married females to be impanelled who soon discovered the truth of the matter. Mary Bateman was duly executed and her body sent for dissection to the surgeons of Leeds Infirmary.

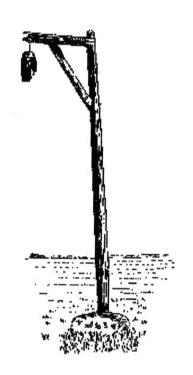

Problem Gentleman

In 1797 *A New Scarborough Guide* was printed in London and dedicated to His Grace John, Duke of Portland. The bye-line on the title page stated that it was "By a Gentleman".

This was not a publishing event of which Scarborough can be proud. The author, that self-styled gentleman, was hanged at Carlisle some years later. It can now be revealed that the gentleman's name was John Hatfield and that he was a first class rogue.

Some five years after the publication of the *Scarborough Guide*, John Hatfield arrived in the Lake District ostensibly on a fishing holiday. He settled himself in a small ale-house near Buttermere kept by a Mr. Robinson. Hatfield had taken several steps up the social ladder since the *Scarborough Guide* days and had now become the Hon. A.A. Hope, member for Dumfries.

Thinking that he might be able to repair his dilapidated finances by a suitable marriage, he set about the conquest of a moneyed lady who was holidaying in the Lake District. Fortunately for the lady her friends must have rumbled him and warned her against him, because nothing came of it. Thrown back on his heels he made up to the landlord's daughter, Mary. She must have been an attractive girl because she was known locally as the Maid of Buttermere.

Here he was more successful. She, dazzled no doubt by the thought of marrying into the aristocracy, fell for his blandishments, as they say in the best novels of the period. They were married in the Parish Church on October 2nd, 1802.

Having thus established himself with the locals, John began cashing in. He seems to have been able to persuade a number of people to cash his drafts on the grounds that he was far away from his own banking house. Having collected a respectable sum he left on what was to have been an extended honeymoon. However, he must have quickly run through the money, because he was soon back. But now retribution was treading on his heels. He heard that a warrant had been granted for his arrest and decided that it was time for him to move on.

Even at this stage someone was gullible enough to cash one of his phoney drafts. With this money in his pocket he got across the lake and away on the pretext of going fishing. Poor Mary was left with his few belongings, amongst which was an old tin trunk containing documents disclosing what was later to be described as a "dark tissue of crimes". Among the papers was the certificate of a previous marriage.

The M.P. Colonel Hope, whose name Hatfield had borrowed, immediately denied that he had married the Maid of Buttermere bigamously or otherwise, and notices to that effect appeared in the press. So did an advertisement offering fifty pounds reward for the apprehension of Hatfield as an imposter, swindler and a felon.

Hatfield was not long at liberty. Having got as far as Brecknock he was taken, brought to London and lodged in

Bridewell. During several examinations at Bow Street, before Sir. R. Ford, a "long course of villainy was brought to light".

However, he was not tried in London but taken to Carlisle and brought before Baron Thompson on August 15th [1802 presumably]. The charges were of having used the name of Hon. Alexander Augustus Hope for fraudulent purposes and of having forged bills under that name.

Neither Mary nor another of his wives could be persuaded to prosecute him for bigamy - not that it would have made any difference to the outcome. He was found guilty as charged and condemned to the gallows.

Being, as we have earlier noted "a gentleman", he is said to have met his death with great calmness and resignation, passing the time after his sentencing in reading, writing and in the offices of religion. It would be interesting to know what he was writing but if it was a guide to the Lake District it has been lost.

As a postscript to a regrettable life it is worth quoting the verse on the title page of John Hatfield's opus:
"No party lies I herald for the press,
But modest truth in artless English dress."

Yorkshire

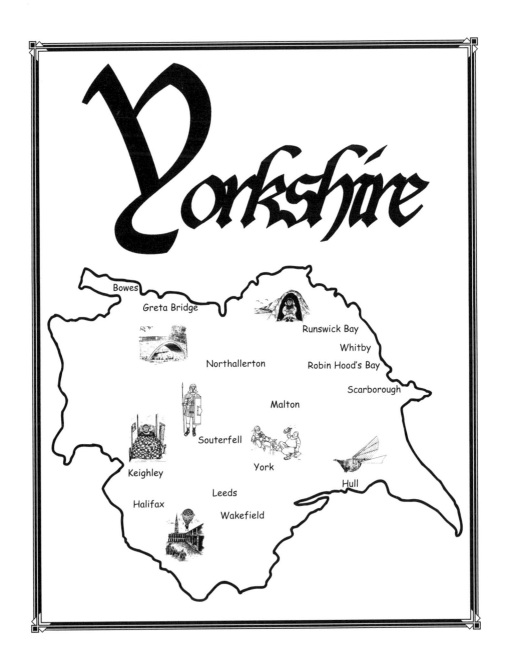

Bowes

Greta Bridge

Runswick Bay

Northallerton

Whitby

Robin Hood's Bay

Scarborough

Malton

Souterfell

York

Keighley

Hull

Leeds

Halifax

Wakefield

Problem Family

Robin Horton was by trade a chimney-sweep. He operated in the district around Northallerton about the year 1765. Incredible though it seems, he had two club feet, his wife one club foot and he had a grey horse which also had a club foot. Apart from his club feet, for which he cannot really be blamed, he does not seem to have been at all prepossessing either in looks or in character. He is described as being a person tall and ruffianly with manners which were revolting. His wife also was of "a most disgusting appearance" and with depraved habits. His two sons and a daughter all appear to have shared in the family characteristics.

Despite this, Horton appears to have had a good connection as a sweep at all the large houses for miles around Northallerton. He always travelled to his work with the grey club-footed horse. Also, it is recorded that the pair, horse and man, were frequently seen setting out after dark on errands about which the sweep was noticeably reticent. And they were often seen returning in the early hours by unfrequented paths.

These nocturnal excursions aroused some suspicions in the Northallerton townsfolk, suspicions which they kept to themselves in view of the dangerous aspect and reputation of the Hortons.

Then, one winter when the snow lay thick upon the ground, the mansion of a wealthy gentleman, a few miles from Northallerton, was broken into and a quantity of plate and other valuables was stolen. The affair does not argue any great degree of intelligence in the Hortons, for the law officers soon found impressions of club feet around the house. They were able to follow horse's tracks right back to the Hortons' house.

Horton and his two sons were taken up and, after examination by a local magistrate, were committed to York for trial. One of the sons turned King's evidence and Horton and the other son were transported for life.

The remaining son returned home and continued to work as a sweep, but most people were loathe to employ him because of the family's shocking reputation, so he got little work. Nevertheless, the family seemed to prosper and lacked for nothing. Yet it was some time before anything definite could be proved against them. Then, one night, mother, son and daughter were all caught breaking into the house of a titled lady. The club-footed horse was standing nearby waiting to carry home the spoils. To everyone's relief, all three were transported and the horse shot.

Ecclesiastical Arguments II:

The Bloody Battle for Fish at Hornsea Mere

In the summer of 1260 there came to a head a long-standing dispute between the Abbot of St. Mary's Abbey, York and the Abbot of Meaux. Both these reverend gentlemen claimed the right of fishing in the southern part of Hornsea Mere. It was no laughing matter, for it was of the utmost importance to keep the monks in one's care well fed on fast days. Who knows what sins the brethren might fall into if their bellies were quite empty. Fish, report tells us, was their staple substitute for the beef, venison and fat capons which were on the table on the days when they were not fasting, or, at least, were on the Abbot's table.

In the days of trial by combat it is not surprising that the two prelates, when they had exhausted their fund of verbal slings and arrows, should bethink them of putting the matter to the test of sword and battle-axe. Although it may seem rather a pity that the two prelates did not indulge in a bout of fisticuffs, single sticks or even swordplay, custom merely demanded that they should appoint champions to fight for them. God would then decide who was in the right. As the historian Hallam tells us: "In all doubtful cases the Combat was awarded and God, as they deemed, was the judge."

So it was that on a summer day in the year 1260 there was gathered a great and jolly crowd of the inhabitants of Hornsea and neighbourhood. The spectators were in holiday mood, for not often did they have the opportunity of watching a battle without having to fight in it. The two prelates, comfortably mounted on their palfreys and surrounded by their retinue, paced about keeping well clear of each other, while the champions prepared themselves for battle. There were six (some say seven) champions on either side and they were soon ready, lined up opposite each other in the ring which had been marked out on the Mere side. They were armed with pointless swords, hammers or jointed maces and were, of course, all clad in the armour of the time and carried shields.

The herald sounded his trumpet and the Marshall signed for the battle to begin. With a great crashing and thumping the two sides came together, maces and hammers whirling and swords slashing. Hubert, York's special champion, took a sickening wallop on the head and went down amid groans from his supporters. As he tried to get back onto his feet Brian of Meaux brought his weapon down with a massive thump onto the dazed man's shield and down again went Hubert. But help was at hand. Two York lads rushed in and straddled Hubert until he recovered and scrambled to his feet.

Meanwhile a couple of Meaux boys were laying into John of the Ouse who was forced back. Sweating and bleeding, the champions struggled back and forth. Then Hubert got annoyed and, flinging his shield at one of his opponents, felled him. William of Atwick of the Meaux side also flung away his shield and, whirling the heavy studded ball at the end of his mace, rushed right into the York lines, leaving two prostrate combatants behind him. However, John of the Ouse wasn't having this and, picking William up bodily, flung him back among his mates. The trumpet sounded for the end of round one.

After a rest and a flagon of ale all the champions were still on their feet, if not quite so full of the fighting spirit as before. Round two began. Once more the crashing and battering blows fell thick and fast. So it was for rounds three and four and so on until evening, neither side having gained any real advantage, and now the well-blooded combatants were much the worse for a hard day's wear. Then the Yorkists, annoyed by the taunts of some of the monks from Meaux, decided it was now or never and summoned all their remaining energy. Hubert, raging like a demon, picked up one of the Meaux boys and threw him clean out of the ring thus, by the rules, putting him out of the fight. Then the York lads charged the remaining five and demolished them in a ruin of broken shields, blood and broken heads. The battle was over and York had triumphed. The surprising thing was that only one of the combatants, a Meaux man, died later of his wounds.

The herald's trumpet sounded again and the Justician, Roger of Thurkelby, gave his decision: the victory and the fishery was York's. The monks of Meaux would have to look elsewhere for fish to fill their capacious bellies on meatless days.

N.B. Tradition tells us that the Abbey of Meaux, or Melsa, owed its foundation to the problems of an over-portly nobleman, William le Gros, Earl of Albermarle and Lord of Holderness. The Earl had done something to displease Mother Church and was ordered by the Pope to make a pilgrimage, on foot, to Jerusalem to expiate his sins. As the good Earl was so fat he could scarcely waddle, the prospect of such a journey could hardly have appealed to him. He objected and was absolved on condition that he would build an Abbey. This must have seemed like a reasonable alternative as he would only have to supply the money and let somebody else do the work. So Meaux was built some six miles north of Hull.

It was a foundation which never seemed to prosper. There must have been some kind of mania which passed from abbot to abbot - a fatal fascination for litigation. The place was several times ruined by law suits.

Circumstantial though it sounds, the tale of the battle at Hornsea Mere is probably largely fabrication. Other records show that the dispute, when it occurred, was actually settled by combat, but that the trial took place at York and was between two champions only. Swords and maces are unlikely weapons anyway: the usual weapon was a long-handled hammer with a leather shield for protection.

Yorkshire

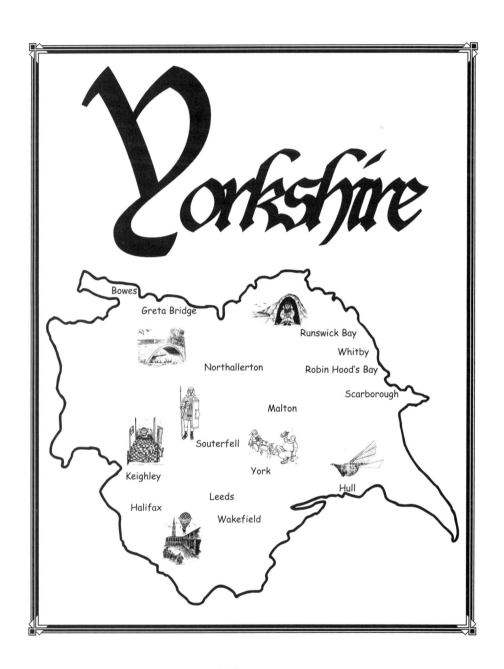

Bowes

Greta Bridge

Runswick Bay

Whitby

Northallerton

Robin Hood's Bay

Scarborough

Malton

Souterfell

Keighley

York

Hull

Leeds

Halifax

Wakefield

The Siege of Forcegarth

In the seventeenth century Stainmoor and Upper Teesdale were pretty wild parts. Stainmoor was the haunt of bands of robbers who were able to disappear into its fastnesses to escape any pursuit after their crimes. It was at the Spital Inn, which still stands by the busy roadside between Bowes and Brough, that one of these gangs was foiled in an attempt to use the Hand of Glory. But that is another story. There is, incidentally, a fine specimen of the Hand of Glory in Whitby Museum.

Forcegarth is a farm near High Force in Teesdale. There has been a farm at this place since the early sixteenth century or before. The farmhouse itself has been rebuilt in a slightly different position from where it stood at the time of this tale. In its earlier days it would have been a low, thatched house with small mullioned windows and strong oaken door studded with nails, strongly hinged and with a massive bar which dropped into slots in the wall on the inside. Such fortifications were needed.

A family called Hutchinson lived at Forcegarth for many years and one of them, or more probably one of their successors, the Robinsons, was, in addition to farming the place, in business as a local carrier. One of his clients wished to have some gold transported in payment for business transactions. So, without telling the carrier the real nature of the package, he put the gold in an iron pot, covered it well and labelled it "Horse-shoe nails".

There must have been a leakage in security somewhere, for a band of robbers then operating from Stainmoor must have heard rumours that the carrier was to be in possession of a valuable cargo and hoped to be able to help themselves. It seems strange that they did not simply waylay the carrier and search his cart, but for some reason they made their attack on the farmhouse.

As was his custom on his rounds, the carrier was expected to spend the night at Forcegarth before carrying on and delivering the goods the next day. Something delayed him, and he did not arrive in the evening as expected but the band must have thought he would be there. They surrounded the house and attempted to break in. Only the carrier's wife and two maidservants were in the house and they had the door barred before the attack started and the robbers could not get in.

When the carrier arrived the following morning he realised that a further attack might be made. The door was barred early and they sat down to wait. Sure enough, at about midnight, sounds of several men moving about and talking were heard and then there was a violent attack on the door. When this was unsuccessful they turned to the windows. At this the carrier got down his blunderbuss which he had loaded in readiness and fired out of the window which was under attack. There was a shriek and a volley of curses from outside and then another violent attack on the front door. Finally they gave up and went away and the rest of the night passed quietly.

When it was light the carrier, his blunderbuss reloaded, went nervously outside. In the yard he found a patch of blood and then a bloody trail as if a body had been dragged along. It led to the pool below High Force and there it ended. It seemed that the gang had consigned a dead companion to the river and then gone off from such a dangerous neighbourhood. There is even a tale that the dead robber haunts the pool below High Force, although he does not seem to have been heard of lately.

The cream of the whole story is that the gold for which a man had died and a robber band discomfited had not been in the house at all. It had spent the night in the midden where the carrier had dumped it, thinking it was of little value.

Yorkshire

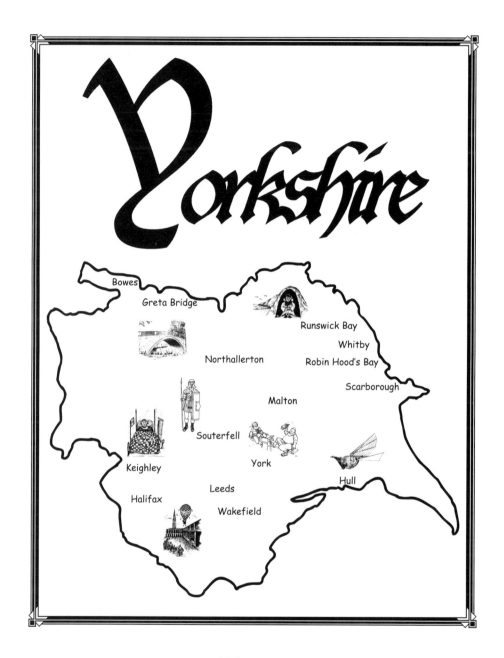

Bowes

Greta Bridge

Runswick Bay

Whitby

Northallerton

Robin Hood's Bay

Scarborough

Malton

Souterfell

York

Keighley

Hull

Leeds

Halifax

Wakefield

THE ADVERTISERS

From a window poster in a Halifax shop about 1852.

151

DR. JOHN TAYLOR

The reputed water Doctor from Sheffield
gives his advice gratis by casting the morning urine, on
any complaint whatsoever incident to either Men, Women
or Child. Patients also, who are incapable from infirmity of
attending in person upon Dr. John, by forwarding their
urine may have advice gratis.

The Doctor now has the pleasure to announce that
he will attend The Jolly Butcher Inn, Whitby every fortnight
on Saturday. No personal attendance upon families under
the fee of one guinea.

DR. JOHN

has found by practical experience, that HERBS of the
field have always proved the best medicine for relieving
afflicted bodies, & eradicating disorders of ever so long
standing when all others fail. Dr. John is in the possession
of worms from five to sixty-five feet in length, which have
come from different patients under his care. There follows a
number of letters of apppreciation from which we take the
following:-

*"Mrs. Simpson, wife of Mr. Simpson, farmer of
Slatepit Dale, near Chesterfield, through the efficacious
Medicine of Dr. John of Sheffield voided on the 27th of
March 1815 a surprising tape worm measuring in length
upward of thirty yards and containing 3,050 joints. This
wonderful cure was performed in the short space of two
days, after having been under the first medical aid for six or
seven years."*

From a poster. Circa 1817.

TREMENDOUS SENSATION
ROARS OF LAUGHTER

For two nights only.
The Temperance Hall, Whitby
August 30th & 31st

PROFESSOR CHADWICK
Begs to announce that he will perform his
WONDERFUL, ASTOUNDING & AMUSING EXPERIMENTS
on wakeful human beings illustrating the newly discovered science of **ELECTRIC BIOLOGY** or the science of life. Persons in the wakeful state who come forward voluntarily from the audience, will be operated upon, and will be deprived of the **POWER OF SPEECH, HEARING AND SIGHT!**
Their voluntary motions will be completely controlled so that they can neither rise up nor sit down, except at the will of the operator. Their memory will be taken away so that they will **FORGET THEIR OWN NAME** and that of their most intimate friends. They will be made to stammer, imagine themselves in flames, to feel pain in any part of their body at the option of the operator, that they are lions shewing their teeth and claws, or lambs actually bleating their conviction of the transformation, with many other mental impressions on individuals in a perfectly conscious state. **A WALKING STICK WILL BE MADE TO APPEAR AS A SNAKE & THEY WILL BE MADE DRUNK ON WATER.**

Reserved seats 1s., second seats 6d

From a poster.

153

DR WAITE'S Celebrated Worm Medicine

The word **WORM** in large staring letters having been stuck up in shop windows in this and other towns, whereby the fraternity of

WORM KILLERS,
WORM-DESTROYERS &c,

announce again their various lozenges, powders, plums, &c; it may be necessary to remind the unwary that the use of these multitudinous nostrums have long been superceded by a remedy whose

CERTAINY, INFALLIBILY &
POPULARITY

have been for many years fully established throughout the kingdom, the greater part of Europe & also the continent of America, in the West Indies & on the coast of Africa. The efficacy of which in totally eradicating all disorders occasioned by those horrid vermin called worms, as well as removing such vermin with their cause, has been experienced by & can be witnessed by thousands. It is therefore only necessary to strangers to announce that the popular remedy alluded to is:-

DOCTOR WAITE'S

Celebrated Worm Medicine in the form of gingerbread nuts. Price one shilling per packet.

N.B. One gentleman, named Theophilus Snelling, reports that after trying everything else imaginable, the first dose of Dr. Waite's gave him instant relief by removing the cause of his disorder, and bringing off a large quantity of small worms alive.

From the *Hull Packet* - August 29th 1797.

154

North Country Weather Saws

A thaw wind from the north-east
Robin Hood did detest.   [Yorks]

Hail brings frost in the tail.   [Lancs]

Frost hurts no weeds.

As the day lengthens
So the cold strengthens.   [Yorks]

St. Hilary is the coldest day of the year.   [Jan. 14th. Yorks]

A hoar frost
Third day crost
The fourth lost.   [Lancs]

March borrowed from April
Three days and they were ill,
The one was sleet, the other was snow,
The third was the worst that e'er did blow.

If dry be the buck's horn on Holy Rood morn
'Tis worth a kist of gold,
But if wet be seen ere Holy Rood e'en,
Bad harvest is foretold.   [Yorks]

When the oak leaf curls up
Rain is near.   [Yorks]

If sheep feed uphill in the morning
It is a sign of fine weather.   [Derbyshire]

Rain at Bartholemew-tide christens the potatoes.   [Aug 25th]

If Roseberry Topping wears a cap
Let Cleveland then beware a rap.

If the moon is on its back in the third quarter
It is a sign of rain.

The Cruel Unkle

Squire Solmes lived in Beverley with his wife and infant daughter. He was a very honest gentleman with an income of about 300 pounds a year. When their infant daughter was about two years old the Squire's wife took ill of a fever and died. The Squire was so distressed by the loss of his dear wife that, after mourning her for some two months, he also took a fever.

Realising that he was like to die himself he called to his bedside his only brother, who lived some fourteen miles from town, and said to him:

"Brother, I leave to you the dearest thing I have in the world - my little daughter - and with her I entrust to you my estate. Manage it for her use and take care of her education in virtue and religion, use her as if she were your own and, for my sake, see her married to an honest country gentleman."

His brother faithfully promised the dying man to do all these things and it was not long before Squire Solmes died. His brother, after seeing to the funeral and arranging affairs, took the child home with him and, for a while, used her kindly.

It was not long, however, before it came to his mind that the child was heiress to a good inheritance which could be his but for her presence. His mind dwelt on the matter until he could hardly think of anything else, and he at last determined that he would do away with her. However, he could not bring himself to do her to death so he thought of a scheme whereby he might be eased of her presence and yet, in some sense, salve his conscience against the crime he was committing.

So one day he took her riding with him and, coming to a convenient hollow tree, fastened a gag in the child's mouth so she might not cry out and, consigning her to the depths of the tree, rode away and left her.

Meanwhile, to forestall any gossip which might be aroused by the little girl's disappearance, he made a wax effigy of the child and, laying it in a coffin, gave out that she had been carried off by the same fever that had taken her parents. And so, with much false sorrowing, he had the effigy buried in the churchyard. So he thought himself safe in the inheritance of his brother's property.

It so happened that, shortly after the cruel unkle had ridden off and left his little niece in the tree, another gentleman who was out hunting passed through the wood. He had dreamed the night before that he would see something astonishing when out riding this day. His lady, fearing some mishap, had tried to persuade him not to ride out but he, being anxious to see if there would be a fulfilment of his dream, had ridden out despite her entreaties.

He was riding past the tree which hid the unfortunate child when his horse gave such a start as nearly unseated him. Turning, he saw the hollow in the tree and thought something moved in it. He now recalled his dream and on dismounting soon found something which did indeed astonish him. Inside the hollow he could see the small child looking up at him with imploring eyes. With the help of his man they soon had her out and took the gag from her mouth.

Of course the little girl was not able to tell who she was or what had happened to her. So the gentleman took her home to his wife saying, "See what my dream has brought."

This gentleman and his wife soon came to love the little girl as if she was their own but it was not until Christmas time that they could get any clue as to who she might be. It was near Christmas when an old woman came to their door to sing the Vessel Cups and recognised the child and where she had seen her and that she was supposed to be dead and buried.

The gentleman, being much disturbed by this information, went to the minister of the parish and, after much persuasion, obtained his consent to the child's supposed grave being opened and the effigy was found in it.

The wicked unkle was haled before Mr. Justice Stubbs and, being unable to deny his crime, was committed to the assizes. The Justice appointed the gentleman who had found her the trusteeship of the child and as they had no chick or child of their own they were happy to have her as if she had been their own flesh and blood.

From an old broadsheet.

Acknowledgements

Thanks are due to Elizabeth Woolley for her drawing of Brother Jocundus, and also to Julie Thompson and Jenny Nunn who both contributed specially commissioned line drawings to enhance the text. The remainder of the illustrations belong in the public domain.

I would also like to thank the staff of all of the various archives, museums and repositories consulted during the writing of this book, especially the Whitby Literary and Philosophical Society.